where God walks

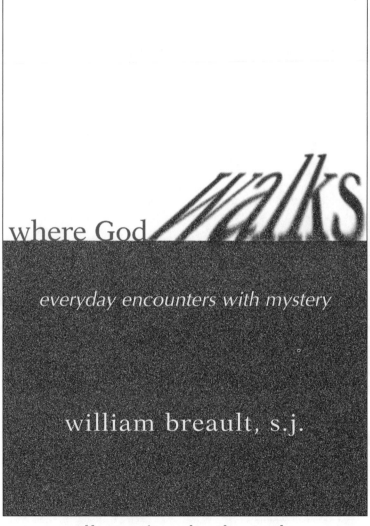

where God *walks*

everyday encounters with mystery

william breault, s.j.

Illustrations by the Author

ave maria press Notre Dame, Indiana

© 2001 by Ave Maria Press, Inc.

International Standard Book Number: 0-87793-710-9

Cover and text design by Katherine Robinson Coleman

Printed and bound in the United States of America.

Library of Congress Cataloging-in-Publication Data
Breault, William.
    Where God walks : everyday encounters with mystery / William Breault.
    p. cm.
    ISBN 0-87793-710-9
    1. God--Knowableness. 2. Experience (Religion) 3. Christian life--Catholic authors. 4. Breault, William. I. Title.
    BT103 .B74 2001
    242--dc21

                                                            00-012071
                                                                 CIP

contents

every book has a spine

"Every book needs a spine."

The meaning of this sentence is quite clear. Without a spine, the pages fall out, and there is no book. What's true of the physical book is also true of its contents. If there is no organizing principle, it, too, falls apart.

After I wrote and rewrote this book a number of times, I asked the publisher, Frank Cunningham, to read it. I have known him for years, both as an editor, and more important, as a friend.

After a few weeks I received a letter from Frank, opened it, and began to read. Frank pointed out that he and another editor, John Kirvan, had read the manuscript. It came as a shock to read what they thought:

> We think there is a book in the material struggling to emerge. Editors talk about a book needing a spine— we don't think you have one for yours yet. It's something beyond the idea of each of these stories revealing how we are touched by God. Both the other reader and I think the spine is you.

No spine to the book? You are the spine? I read the words with some disappointment since initially I had thought the "spine" was religious experience. I had missed the obvious. It was, for the most part, about *my* religious experience.

I continued reading the letter with a kind of astonishment, seeing something about myself and the book through the eyes of someone who knew me. The experience was humbling. It brought back memories I had forgotten, or at least had pushed to the back of my mind.

> Some years ago you told me you thought your ministry was to listen to people, to be present to and for them. Am I remembering correctly? I think so. . . . You have a gift for drawing people out.

Had I said that? The wheels of memory began turning. I recalled earlier days of listening to nature while walking through the giant redwoods in a storm, wondering what it would feel like to be strapped high on a redwood, to feel what it felt during the storm. It was the same with the ocean. What would it feel like to be thrown into a dangerous, rock studded ocean during a storm and manage to spend the whole night there? And live through it? What an experience of the ocean that would be!

That same experience began to happen with people. I wanted to enter into their lives, see through their eyes, look at life from their viewpoint. So, I started to listen carefully to what others were saying.

For years I listened as a *conscious* act, even to people I didn't feel much affection for. But then, listening as a consciously performed act seemed to stop. Perhaps it had become part of me.

Frank's letter brought these memories back. With no little embarrassment, I read on:

> You've listened to us one-by-one in the context of an ever-present God who knows us intimately. So now, after years of listening, you have accumulated a lot of stories. Tell them. Don't let them tell themselves. *You* tell them. Reveal their power. Your point in relating these stories is the passing on of God's love.

He was offering me a spine and an approach to the book.

Your commentary [on the stories] should illustrate the idea of the Irish poet Paul Murray, who observes that God loves us so much that if we were all to self-destruct, God would die of loneliness. You want to help us [the readers] recognize how God touches our lives with that love.

After reading the letter, I called Frank and objected to being the spine of the book. "It's a little like standing naked in public. It's a bit scary," I protested. His response surprised me:

"Scary? Sure. But sometimes it's fun to run around naked!"

I interpreted this to mean, "Take a chance."

With that kind of encouragement, I had to decide whether I wanted to be the spine of the book. If that were the whole of it—simply to expose my own inner life in public—I would have given up the idea. But, what if there is *something* in the very nature of religious experience, in the very nature of Mystery that touches us all? What if all religious experience is *only* about God touching our lives with love? If so, then certainly sharing mine might be worth the risk.

Having decided it might be worth the risk, I had to give some thought to that "something"—*my* religious experience.

But I hesitated again. When I wondered why, I became painfully aware of what I believe is at the center of my own personality: desire and fear; desire for adventure, for what is new, for beauty, for the mysterious, for God—but fear also, which seems to be a result of desire. Fear of being seen as angry with God, or fearful of God; fear of making mistakes and being seen as a failure. It is difficult to put such things down on paper for others to read. I don't mind people knowing I desire, but must they know that I fear? This is what really held me back. I didn't want to be exposed. But how else can I talk about religious experience, about Mystery?

So, I take a risk in writing this book. I hope it's a worthwhile one.

In taking the risk, let me say right from the start that I prefer using the expression "the experience of *Mystery*" rather than "*religious* experience." Religion is so often associated with a particular set of doctrines, rules, and institutional structures. There are no such things present in the experience of Mystery. It is a moment of freedom, expansiveness; a movement outside of the normal state we're usually in, i.e., the dedicated preoccupation with one's self.

The encounter with Mystery sweeps me out of the tight focus in which my ego ordinarily operates—so aware of itself as the center of *the* universe. And it always catches me off guard, stealing past my careful defenses, disarming me. Sometimes it is awesome, sometimes humorous. In every single instance, I know I am being addressed. Of course, this can be disconcerting. It is clear proof that things are not under my control.

Furthermore, the experience of Mystery is purely personal. It is certainly not something I was trained to expect; it wasn't taught in school, except indirectly in poetry, music, and art. It comes with living, with life—and always without warning, always a surprise, even if it lasts for only a moment.

I believe Mystery ties people together, moves within and between them. It sings through nature and calls out from the stars. It creates and addresses us. Above all, it is the presence of Beauty which I find impossible to pin down. It just doesn't fit into my neat, chiseled-out categories. Nor will it stay put! "The wind blows where it chooses, and you hear the sound of it, but you do not know where it comes from or where it goes" (Jn 3:8).

Speaking as an artist for a moment, one can approach the viewing of a painting as though staring *at* an object. A *voyeur* might enjoy looking at a picture of Diana in Her Bath. He or she is at a safe distance. One can approach life in the same way, as though looking at an object. But the moment Diana looks back—that's an encounter! And a

10   where God walks

mysterious one! So it is with the Mystery at the heart of life. When it speaks, it is always Subject to Subject.

This book, then, is about such personal encounters, not just in my life, but in the lives of friends who have honored me by sharing what has touched them deeply, and therefore touched me.

At some level
Deeper than the surface
We see.
It all fits together
And shines
Brilliantly.

On rare occasions
The facade dissolves;
Then we see
Right into the center—
And gasp
With surprise!

This is grace,
An attraction,
A given:
The Mystery at the heart of life
Makes a sign,
Giving itself to us
In a non-mistakable, conscious way.
And for one moment
We stand still,
Rooted in that encounter,
Staring in disbelief,
Holding our masks
In our hands.

All too soon
We shall put them on again,
Though the fit
Will never be the same.

the novice tree

At the age of twenty-three, I found myself in a seminary. I say "found" because I wasn't really sure how I got there. Nothing in my background pointed to the priesthood. The idea never entered my mind. My interests had always been direct and focused on material success and marriage. Marriage was important. The idea of living without a woman and a family struck me as absurd. I dreamed of a house, a wife, and children, a dream shaped by Hollywood movies.

I took a job early in life and then enlisted in the Army Air Corps in the Second World War and was trained to be a B-29 gunner. But my experience of violence in military service shook me enough that my dreams started to fade. I began to question my own life, realizing that if I continued on the path I was experiencing in military life, I would become what I appalled.

I couldn't even guess what a new path would be. I was like a shipwrecked sailor at sea with nothing to hold on to but the sea itself! So I prayed. When asked why he prayed, someone once gave a short, swift response: "So I can feel I'm not alone." I prayed for the same reason.

I prayed to keep my sanity. I prayed for inner peace. I prayed to get back home. I even made promises: "Get me home, Lord, safe and sane, and I promise you, I'll go to a good Catholic college, marry a good Catholic girl, and raise a good Catholic family." I thought this was a bargain God couldn't resist.

When I returned home and got out of the Air Corps, the first thing I did was buy a motorcycle and enroll in Loyola University in Los Angeles. The name meant nothing to me, but some of the men who taught there soon did. They called themselves Jesuits, and they impressed me by their lives and intelligence. I was barely past my teenage years, and they were the first adults I met who seemed to know something about life. They had a sense of direction. I had none.

The influence of my teachers on me was subtle— sometimes. At other times, it was blatantly direct. I say this because of one man in particular—a great-bodied, good humored Frenchman. His name was Gabriel Menager, and he taught theology.

Once we got to know each other he didn't hesitate to ask me, "What are you going to do with your life?" Of course, I had no answer. I was trying to figure that out myself!

One day, as I parked my motorcycle on campus, he spotted me and shouted, "Well, Saint Paul, what are you waiting for? A bolt of lightning from the heavens? When are you going to get off that motorcycle?" What he meant, I came to understand through this and other such comments, was, "When are you going to become a Jesuit?"

It was flattering to a twenty-year-old who had barely gotten through high school; who, in fact, was advised to leave. Nevertheless, I saw his comments as pressure and told him so. "I wish you would stop saying things like that. It ruins friendships and makes me feel like an idiot in front of the guys. I have no desire to become a priest. I intend to get married, and have a big family."

This produced the desired effect, temporarily. He became contrite, promised never to embarrass me again— yet repeated it the next time he saw me!

He had me targeted, and I found it disturbing. I don't like being a target; nor did I like the psychology he used—

14   where God walks

keep repeating something long enough and it will finally sink in and produce fruit. It was hardly an invitation; I saw it as pressure and maybe even extortion! He was telling me, "Why don't you recognize what God put there? I can see it. Why can't you?"

A few years passed during which I started a successful business painting tennis courts. After a while the work started to bore me. I needed more of a challenge and the old malaise precipitated by my military experience returned. Where was I going in life? What was I supposed to do? What was life about? Where was the ideal woman, the all-absorbing success I sought?

A priest, whom I don't remember now, suggested I make a three-day retreat to get some insight, maybe some help from God. I suspect he was hoping for more and saw my struggles as hopeless resistance to the inevitable. I was willing, but cautious. Maybe God *would* enlighten me. Maybe he would help me figure out what my life was about and where I fit in.

I had no idea what a retreat was, except that it was made in silence and someone gave talks.

This one was a disaster! Everywhere I turned there were crosses, grim faced retreat masters, silent people walking around like mummies, and talks on heaven, hell, death, judgment, and Jesus Christ saving us all from one another. After one day, I broke the retreat schedule by staying out late at night and sneaking in after lights out.

After two days, it was clear to the people in charge that I didn't belong there. After three, I went home with stunningly clear thoughts: never again would I make a retreat. Nor would I become a priest. That had been decided once and for all. I felt giddy with the realization that while I had been open to the idea, God had let me know it was not my path to walk. I had tried but was, happily, found wanting.

Three months later, I entered the seminary.

What happened? I've never been quite sure. Somehow I was able to hear an invitation and overcome the ambiguity.

A novitiate is the first year or two of seminary life where one begins formation in the spiritual life. It's an intense experience, and in those days students rarely left the novitiate.

Two months after I entered, my mother died and I was allowed to leave and attend her funeral. It was a very sad time for me, but my companions I left behind were making bets that "once I saw the world again" I would never return. I did, however. I had seen enough of the so-called "world."

Immediately after returning from my mother's funeral, I started one of the great Jesuit experiences: the silent, thirty-day retreat! Imagine my apprehension as I approached that experiment, so soon after my mother's death. The subject would be death, heaven and hell, judgment and repudiation of the body. I thought of my mother, only forty-two years old, stiff and cold in her coffin. These were not thoughts that led to a feeling of friendliness toward God, or to confidence in the decision I had made to enter the novitiate!

As the retreat continued, new ideas, concepts, feelings, and doubts filled my mind. Many of them were negative or intimidating; for example, the idea that I had been created and was being held in existence that very moment by the will of God. That was a scary thought for someone who thought he was independent.

After one week of silence, the retreatants got a day off to breathe and get ready for the next week. But this time I was depressed and anxious. I thought I had made the right choice, but I certainly wasn't at peace, as the rest of the seminarians seemed to be.

Maybe the novitiate wasn't the place for me. Maybe the whole thing was a pious illusion, a way of choosing a profession guaranteed to give me the success I wanted. People looked up to and respected priests, after all. Maybe my decision to enter had nothing at all to do with God.

With that depressing thought I sat on a bench under a great oak overlooking sloping grape fields and a cluster of new homes. In the branches of the tree, the birds were having nothing to do with my negative mood. They were happily chattering and singing away, while I looked down the slope to the young married people who had recently purchased homes. There I watched a common scene: a car would drive up, park, and a young man would spring out and greet his lovely wife standing in the doorway. It was just like the movies.

And here I was, on the hill wrestling with life and death, salvation and damnation, freedom and the lack of it! What a startling difference!

Old questions came back to haunt me. Was I a glutton for punishment? Was this really my life? My choice? What was I doing here? Was it *my* decision to enter, or had I sold out to the flattering pressure and expectations of others? Had I bought into it for my own reasons? I even wondered if maybe God had taken advantage of me.

I wanted to be the one who was greeted at the door by a lovely woman—not the one sitting under an oak tree, dressed in *black*, filled with *black* thoughts, and listening to *black* birds chattering away.

My mind was racing so fast that I found myself saying out loud: "God! Give me a sign and I'll get out of this place right now."

While saying this, I stood up. The quick and unexpected motion frightened the birds above me. They all took flight simultaneously, and as they did, they evacuated themselves. Suddenly it was snowing! And I was covered with it, all over my head, my shoulders, and the sleeves of my clothes.

Startled, I was caught totally unaware. Eyes wide open—mouth too, for that matter. Then I burst out laughing. I got just what I had asked for, a sign, but what a sign! "Oh come on! Don't take yourself so seriously. Loosen up a little," seemed to be the message.

My depression and anxiety evaporated and were replaced with affirmation, wonder, even joy.

Do I think that God interceded into the natural order of events and got all the birds to fly off at the same time, interfere with their digestive systems in such a way that I got snowed on? I have no idea. God is far too immense and beyond my comprehension—though I never give up trying to understand!

What I do know for certain is that I asked for a sign—which I rarely do—and received a *tangible* sign. In that moment, I sensed God not as off at some great distance, but intimately present and with a sense of humor.

The real question, however, that seems to explain what happened to me as a *religious* experience is this: Why did I burst out laughing instead of gloomily saying to myself: "There's your sign. You asked for it. You just got it! Now you know what God really thinks of you"?

Such a scenario would have been right in line with my thinking, a fitting end to a day of depression and anxiety. Instead, I burst out laughing, and that made what seemed insurmountable, so depressing and big, *diminish* and disappear.

In that same moment, I felt the intimate closeness of God—not in a way I had ever expected. Rather, God seemed so close that he knew just what would make me laugh with surprise. Anything that has that kind of power is beyond my control.

Furthermore, like all good humor, it was unexpected, completely turning my self-questioning around in such a way that I could instantly view myself objectively. I call this grace. It's a little like looking in a mirror when feeling sad and disheartened and seeing your own image staring back, laughing, radiant, and fearless.

I can only explain this in terms of an encounter: Person to Person, Subject to Subject.

the God who walks
with people

About ten years ago, I met a young pastor who also served as the director of religious education for his diocese. While I was visiting his parish, giving a retreat for his parishioners, I ran across a flyer advertising the diocese's first annual religious writing contest, open to everyone in the diocese. The priest-director thought up this idea after studying the prayers and creative liturgies that children wrote. He reasoned that if such talent existed among the children, why not have a diocesan-wide religious writing contest, with prizes for those works which were above average? He even planned to print a small brochure in which some of the poetry and other types of writing would be displayed.

Close to a thousand people—not all of them children—entered the contest! There were poems from first graders as well as from adults with graduate degrees. And it was not a small brochure that was published, but a book of thirty pages.

When I was given a copy, I flipped through it rapidly without paying too much attention to the cover. I was interested in the contents.

What a variety of material was sent in, especially from children! A second grader wrote about being in the world:

> I would like to be a bird
> And fly across the sky.
> I would build a nest to sleep in.
> I would look up at the sky
> And pray to God with my song.

Another child in the fifth grade wrote about how she sees and feels God:

> When I see beautiful flowers,
> I see God. When I see all
> The animals and the fruit
> On the trees,
> I see God.
> I think of how God created
> All living things.
>
> I feel God is always with me.
> Sometimes I look up into the
> Sky and feel that God is
> Looking at me and is smiling.

As I looked at the children's poetry, I smiled at their naiveté, as though seeing God in the life around them were a simple phase they were going through because they were children. They would outgrow it, I thought.

But at the same time, I felt a tinge of envy. I even found myself wishing the children who wrote these poems would never grow up, but would hold on to that innocent and believing wonder.

So, I experienced a mixture of admiration and conde-scension. In the back of my mind was the cynical thought: Wait till they grow up and encounter the real world, then we'll see what kind of poetry they write.

I closed the book.

It was at that moment that I noticed the cover. It was a drawing, done by a fifth grader, of an orange and black figure with a large basketball-sized head, and a thin

tube-like neck joined to a square body, from which projected two pipe-cleaner legs and two rather fat arms. The feet
on the legs were both pointed in the same direction. The
hands were wide open and facing the viewer. On the left
arm there was a black wristwatch.

It was a picture of God!

What surprised me was not the simple, child-like con-
ception of God as one like us, walking with us, seeing out
of human eyes, hearing with human ears, and wearing a
wristwatch. No, it was something else, almost disturbing—
the way in which the figure was treated by the young artist.

Most of us are born with two eyes, two ears, a mouth,
two legs, and two arms. This painting, however, showed
God with only one of each: one eye, wide open and staring
straight ahead. The other—what there was of it—was simply a small dot surrounded with a scrawl of writing which
said: "God sees people." One ear was perfectly formed. In
place of the other ear, there was more writing: "God listens
to people." The ear was missing, as if it had been altogether worn away!

There was no mouth to this God, but in place of the
mouth, written in orange, were the words: "God talks with
people." Although there were two legs, one was only an
interrupted, single thin line which wavered as it
approached a word connecting it to the body: "God walks
with people."

The price for God seeing, listening, talking, and walking with people was, in the mind of this fifth grader, a God
who lost something of himself by giving it. His ear was
worn off from listening to those he loved. His eye was
burned out from seeing. His mouth had ceased to exist, and
he walked on one leg, for the other had been given away.

The insight of this child started me thinking about the
enclosure that seems to surround children, protecting
them, making it natural for them to believe. I had always
seen it as a lack of something, a lack of growth, maturity,
realism, a web of unreality that is brushed away with ado-
lescence. Yet I found myself longing to enter once more into
that world. I suddenly realized that the web was on my

side, made up of layer after layer of ambition, good works, and the desire to please others.

That child's intelligence was wide open to mystery, which she sensed intuitively, as an artist would. Mine was far more focused, determined, trying to figure out where I was going in life, what I wanted to achieve and accomplish—to get, in other words.

The whole experience was a wake-up call.

Astounding! That the darkest mystery in life, the unanswered question of why the innocent suffer and die, a question that often turns people into atheists, the young girl answered with a crayon: God is in it.

It was a humbling experience for someone with five degrees representing years of study about God.

I rehashed a lot of ideas that were pounded into my head since I was a child: the belief that God imposes suffering to satisfy his justice, that he is invulnerable and cannot be touched by our pain.

I'd be a liar to say I haven't asked God, either out loud or in prayer, "Why? Why do you allow such suffering to go on?"

This is a question that can eventually destroy trust and faith. But it never entered this child's mind, since she saw suffering not as coming from God; instead, she saw God entering into suffering.

She depicted God as vulnerable, able to suffer, and with us.

Jewish sages have taught that God went into exile once he created man and woman. He is hidden, in other words. And I believe it! So, too, did the fifth-grade artist.

But for her, God is hidden in flesh! I believe this, blindly. The child-artist grasped it intuitively.

As a priest, I teach this: that God's love drove him into flesh and the predictable result was suffering, the passion, death, and resurrection. As long as there is flesh, this movement of God into flesh continues. So does the suffering.

I was so moved by the child's insight that I took the book with me, cut off the cover, and carried it wherever I went, in order to tell her story to as many as I could.

toyo

After a serious illness I got an unexpected recompense—
recuperation in Hawaii for two months! Since I love swim-
ming and the finest beaches in the world were only fifteen
minutes away, this was an easy thing to do.

One day during my stay there, a local friend asked if I'd
like to visit the outer island of Molokai. To be more precise,
he wanted to visit Kalapapaa, the leper colony at the tip of
Molokai made famous by Damien DeVeuster, a nineteenth-
century Belgian priest who lived and died there. Before
Damien's arrival, Kalapapaa had been virtually a prison, a
place of abandonment for the rejects of society. Because
there was no law or order, the lepers lived there amidst fear
and violence. Damien changed all that.

I had mixed feelings about going to Kalapapaa. I had
had my own brush with death and had undergone major
surgery. I didn't want to see sickness in others and was
repelled by leprosy. On the other hand, I was attracted to
the person of Damien and decided to make the trip.

It was a disturbing flight on a small plane, evidently
designed to bump through the air. At one point I thought
the pilot had lost control. We were flying low over the sea,
heading directly toward a cliff that rose three thousand feet
into the air. Below us to our left was a flat, arrow-shaped
peninsula, two and a half miles wide by three miles long. It

projected out into the ocean from the base of the cliff I was sure we were going crash into.

At the last moment the pilot made a sharp left turn into the wind and started to descend onto a very short landing strip. As the plane came closer to the ground, I noticed a sunken ship below the surface of the water. It gave me an eerie feeling.

I also saw the not-too-reassuring sight of a plane that had crashed and was unceremoniously left on the edge of the runway. What little confidence I had was evaporating. A sunken ship and a wrecked plane seemed to foreshadow the death and desolation I might see when I visited the leper colony. But the pilot knew what he was doing and landed us safely.

When I stepped out of the plane, I was struck by how barren the land was and by the constant sound of the sea. My sense of isolation was palpable.

The airport waiting room was divided into two sections: one place for the patients, one for the visitors. It was the same with the restrooms. The message was clear, if unspoken: Don't touch! Don't use anything that had been touched by the patients. All of this under a summer sun in a turquoise sky filled with fleecy, soft clouds moved by the trade winds.

A Belgian priest met me at the airport. He pulled up in a car that looked like it had spent much of its life under water. The salt of the sea air had eaten through the car's enamel, and the dust from the desolate landscape enveloped it.

After talking for awhile, he asked me if I'd like to visit the hospital and talk with the patients. I felt a small rush of fear thinking about it, but I said yes. Maybe it was bravado or the desire to be able to tell others of my experience. Maybe it was something more profound. I'm not sure. At any rate, we drove to the hospital after a tour of the colony, which resembled any small Hawaiian town.

I had previously cut my hand and the wound was open, though I stanched the blood. The Belgian priest noticed the cut and told me in no uncertain terms: "Don't touch the

where God walks

patients!" I stared at him. Was he joking? I had seen enough pictures of people with leprosy, or Hansen's disease as it is now called, and was not about to touch anyone! My reply had nothing to do with the cut on the hand. I feared contagion. In my mind, any kind of contact could communicate the disease.

The first patient I met was sitting in a wheelchair with an autoharp on his lap. How good, I thought, he's still interested enough in life that he wants to learn. Maybe this visit won't be so bad after all. Then I noticed that the man had no fingers. He was pushing down on the steel strings with the knuckles of his two hands. The instrument seemed designed to emphasize his disfigurement. From a distance, I said, "Hello, how are things going?" I also kept my hand in my pocket.

Next I met Tutu. She was a frail, elegant looking woman in her mid-eighties who had spent nearly her whole life in the colony at Kalapapaa. She was sitting in a chair, very still, when we entered her room. I saw marks of the disease on her body, which was clothed in a long Hawaiian dress. The priest introduced me and asked her, "Tutu, this priest just came from San Francisco. Will you sign out the Hail Mary for him?"

Silent and deeply prayerful, Tutu raised her arms and began to sign out the prayer in graceful and slow movements. Confronted with such bright light I felt small.

I also felt less threatened by the disease. This was a human situation, a life sized encounter. Tutu was not a photograph. I thanked her when she finished. She merely nodded and we left the room.

It was obvious to me that Tutu was living on another plane of reality. I felt like an intruder, as though I had disturbed her prayer. But I did leave with a little more confidence, a bit more secure. I was not threatened by what I had seen so far.

All that changed when I opened the door to the next room.

Two women were seated at a table eating. One woman had her back to me, while I looked directly at the face of the other woman, Toyo. I stopped, stunned. The woman had no hair, no eyebrows, no eyes, no nose, no real mouth, and no hands.

She was eating when I entered—but what a chore! Two large cooking spoons had been strapped around her wrists and she scooped up her food from a huge bowl, aiming it at what was once a mouth. The sound of the spoons hitting the bowl filled the air.

My mind was numbed. I couldn't believe anyone so disfigured could still be alive. I wanted to run away.

The priest introduced me, and the clacking sound stopped. Toyo looked in my direction, more to hear than to see. I said something I don't even remember. She responded by unhinging one of the spoons from her right wrist, then pushing the freed stump up and against a hole in her throat. Out came a whistle, resembling a high pitched human word. She sounded like a parrot, or a myna bird, imitating human sounds. "My name is Toyo," she said. I felt like someone had punched me in the stomach. I had trouble breathing—but I understood what she had said.

I looked closely, trying to see the woman through the disease. She had been a Japanese picture bride, I learned later, a beautiful woman who had come to the Islands to marry a wealthy Japanese man. Somewhere during her life she had contracted Hansen's disease and spent the rest of her life in Kalapapaa.

We talked as best we could. I told her where I was living and teaching. Then I asked her a few questions. Nothing very complicated. Toyo's range of interests was not extensive.

When I was about to leave the room, she stopped me and asked for a blessing. I thought of the cut on my hand, but not for long. Something far more important than my fear took over. I laid both hands on Toyo's head and asked God to bless her. It was a spontaneous gesture, free and fearless.

Meeting Toyo had a strong effect on me. She was full of joy. I couldn't understand that. I couldn't understand why she was not depressed. Even if she could see, she had nothing to look at in the mirror. She had lost so much, including her family life, yet she seemed stronger, more at peace than most people I knew.

Perplexed, I wondered what her secret was.

When I returned to Honolulu the question nagged me even more. People there were very conscious of their looks. They dressed smartly and worked hard to shape a world of their own. Many were anxious and fearful, trying to get many of the things Toyo had been forced to give up.

I was struck by the enormous contrast, one that has stayed with me for years, just as her image has.

To this day I wonder what force within her was stronger than the loss of beauty, a disfigurement so severe that people would find her revolting. She was ostracized socially, set apart from the normal things that give people pleasure. The casual onlooker might take a quick look and pass her by as some kind of vegetative growth.

Her disease had humbled her.

Yet she was joyful! How does one explain such a thing?

hospital chaplain

I just received a note that a friend of mine is very sick and close to death. She is a person who had been very much misunderstood throughout her religious life because of a disease not properly diagnosed.

I first met her in a hospital in a large city. She was suffering great darkness and a sense of abandonment—yet her faith was strong, so much so that she offered her life for a single woman with five children who was undergoing great misfortunes.

Her room was bare, empty of the usual machines. Just a bed, a lamp, and a nearby table. On the table was a paper cup with a straw in it. I was told later that anything that could possibly be used as a weapon had been removed. The woman was thought to be suicidal.

She didn't look suicidal to me. She looked scared.

We talked awhile. I saw there was a question in her eyes, as though she wondered just how far she could trust me. I was, after all, a stranger, even if I were the chaplain.

The conversation stayed on a light level. I asked questions about what was wrong with her, why she was in the hospital—she looked healthy enough!

I was making an attempt to be humorous. It didn't quite succeed. I got evasions for answers. "I'm here for tests. The doctors are trying to determine what is wrong with me."

The next evening, and each evening after, I stopped by her room, till gradually some level of trust began to develop between us. And just as gradually, she began to tell me of her experience with a disease that others didn't understand, or were unwilling to admit was real.

She had been experiencing great fatigue for quite some time, and more recently light dizzy spells, which were interpreted by others as signs of laziness, an excess of self-love. Some believed she was using fatigue as an excuse to get out of teaching class, or at least to cut down on her teaching schedule. Unable to communicate with those around her, since she didn't know herself what was wrong, she began to suspect her own balance. Her fears increased!

She continued to teach, but the dizzy spells kept recurring. She became more and more anxious. Finally, out of desperation, she went to see a young priest for guidance. This was interpreted, at that time, as a further sign that she was off-balance, maybe even something more. Rumors multiplied. Perhaps she was psychotic! She was ordered to have shock treatments, but they didn't help her.

Finally she ended up in the hospital. Doctors continued to attempt to determine exactly what was wrong with her, yet by many others she was treated as though the whole thing were a product of her imagination. Imagine the desperation, the fear, and the sense of uselessness this woman felt.

She became very depressed, and the thought did enter her mind: "Why don't I just end it all? Oh God! What am I saying?" Once this thought was known, or guessed at, by the medical staff, the room was cleared of anything that could serve as a weapon.

What the woman really needed was compassion. But what she was receiving was the result of fear and ignorance, the fear of her superiors, some of her companions, and even some of the medical staff.

In the well lit, bare room of the hospital she was alone. No one came to visit her. She was convinced she was a misfit, a pariah, an outcast from the human race, for that had been her experience from the onset of the disease.

where God walks

No one spoke Christ to her, I thought. What she needed was the simple reality of his touch. And that is what I did. Each night, after saying a brief prayer—or even during it—I took her hand, then laced my right arm to her left arm, so that skin touched skin. I wanted her to feel the touch of another human being who believed in her, who respected her. There was no resistance. In fact, I thought I detected a small spark of hope, maybe the beginning of trust.

Once the disease, epilepsy, was properly diagnosed and treated, the sister returned to her community. What a reversal took place! Where before they had treated her as mentally unbalanced, her friends now began to look upon her as a martyr. She was esteemed so highly that she was given the care of the young novices entering the order.

This woman had been overloaded with work, wrongly accused, made to suffer the indignity of shock treatments—plus the distrust of her companions and even her superiors; yet I never heard her say one unkind word about anyone. Instead she offered God all she had, her emptiness.

And now she is dying! At the end of a letter firmly written by someone else, telling me of this final sickness, my friend had scrawled a few lines of greeting. They were all but illegible. I quickly wrote a return letter, one she may never read. In it I recalled the times I visited her in the hospital, night after night, to give her courage to live when everything she had ever wished for had been taken from her; a time when she felt abandoned by God and those she knew—and deceived as well. And now she readies herself for the final gift, the passover from this world to Christ!

I prayed for her this evening in a special way. I thought during my prayer that someone special, someone important to our world was leaving, perhaps while I was praying; and the world goes about its regular, even monotonous tasks, as though nothing important were happening.

la petite

A negative mood is a little like an ink stain on a clean, white absorbent cloth: it spreads outward in an ever-widening circle. In just such a mood, I was on a train returning from Lisieux to Paris. I did not want to return to the City of Lights, and to symbolize my unwillingness, I sat with my back toward it. I didn't understand the French people, or their language; I felt extremely self-conscious—and was trying to conceal all these feelings under an impassive mask. I sat bolt upright, staring straight ahead at the back of the train.

The seats immediately around me were empty, but when the train stopped at a small town, three people filled them. Two were elderly ladies. I helped them with their luggage, putting it on the rack above, without speaking a word. When they thanked me, "Merci, monsieur," I merely nodded my head.

I looked upon myself as a stranger in a foreign culture. But I was certain, without any evidence, that everyone on the train knew exactly what I was feeling. Like the ink stain, my bad mood spread, and I very successfully projected my mood onto others. Certainly, I thought, everyone on that train knew I was an American. They must also agree that I was as awkward, out of place, and inept as I felt myself to be. Worse yet, I didn't want to be budged out of my bad mood. In some perverse way, depression can be a warm isolating blanket that keeps others at a safe distance.

A half hour from Paris the train stopped for more passengers. I watched three of them enter the car and walk down the aisle toward me: a plump, middle-aged woman dressed in black, leading two children, a boy of perhaps eleven and a girl of nine. The mother directed the boy to the first available seat, then walked directly toward the two empty seats across the aisle, to my left. The mother took the aisle seat with the little girl next to the window. Across from the pair, and facing them, were two American College students; big, good-looking boys, oblivious of anything but their own culture. They were dressed in short pants. One was reading *Time* magazine; the other was fast asleep with his legs stretched out under the seat the young girl sat on. She pointed this out to her mother, since she had no place to put her legs, but the mother only shrugged her shoulders. What, after all, could be done?

The young girl tried tucking her legs under her, then to the side. Nothing seemed to work. Finally she sat, legs crossed Buddha-like, straight up in the seat and looked out the window. Nothing escaped her gaze. With black, flashing eyes filled with intelligence, she noticed and asked her mother about everything that caught her attention outside the fast moving train.

She had a sharp, engaging attitude overflowing with energy and wonder. She missed nothing. I even felt—or thought I felt—her eyes resting on me, but only for a moment. However, I was conscious of her all the time—and trying not to show it. It's quite an accomplishment to look straight ahead while paying strict attention to what is going on to one's left!

I think I recognized in the young girl the special grace of childhood, a bright new intelligence in the act of discovery: the black eyes, the black hair, and the gestures filled with barely contained excitement—everything about the child interested me. By comparison I felt old and used up, a stranger, and a foreigner as well.

The train stopped once more about ten minutes from Paris. A man getting off left a vacant seat next to the boy, so the mother left the girl to sit with her son for a few minutes. As she moved out of her seat, the young girl occupied it, which put her quite close to me on the aisle to my left. She continued to observe everything around her, including me. I could feel her eyes on me at one point. Within, I was saying something like, "Well, you know she's looking at you, probably wondering about your age, where you're from— who knows what children think about?"

I wanted to turn and look directly at her, but I didn't. Should she say something in French, I'd have to explain, in my stumbling way, that I didn't understand her, or I would have to ask her to please repeat what she had said, but more slowly. What follows is taken from the journal I wrote in that night, once back in Paris:

> I felt the inclination to turn and look at her so strongly, and finally, thank God, I yielded to it. What surprised me was that we were looking directly at each other, eyeball to eyeball! A slow lingering look. No words at all. It must have lasted a good twenty seconds. Then I saw and felt within myself the smile in her eyes before it reached her lips—but it did reach her lips! A smile of understanding, assent, trust—love, really. For one moment on a crowded train to Paris, a smile of love between two strangers, each of whom was a foreigner to the other. A perfect communication. A small and very important mutual gift. A delightful opening into another world, God's world. There was no hurry to the look. It was as looks go, long, a contemplative gaze with no questions. My own face and age were forgotten, as I am sure hers were in that intimate contact. Language at that point would have been interference, disturbing the experience. There is no way to verbally articulate such an experience. It has its own superior language. It was a free act of mutual love and acceptance that transcended time, language,

nationality, and age barriers. I recognized and accepted it as a special gift. Gilbert Keith Chesterton, the English essayist and novelist, said it is no small thing to receive a welcoming smile from someone so recently from God.

A few moments from Paris the train stopped once more and the young girl got up and joined her mother and brother. The three of them left the train. Not a word passed between us. There was no backward glance. The incident seemed closed. But I was no longer depressed, no longer angry. I rode into Paris joyfully—and thought of that experience on the train for the next three days.

I think I was touched by God in this encounter. I had been depressed, unwilling to communicate with those around me, angry and closed in upon myself. Worse, I was projecting these same attitudes on those around me— whom I didn't even know! I was certainly experiencing a negative mood. Actually, "destructive" is a better word to describe it.

I don't believe that negative, destructive moods come from God, for a very simple reason: they are the opposite of the love, peace, and joy God gives to those who are looking for him. In my unexpected communion with the young girl, the negative, destructive feeling was chased out. Wonder and a sense of oneness took its place. Freedom!

The encounter with the little one changed my whole inner atmosphere, and I have never forgotten it. It remains to this day, in my mind, an act of love coming directly from the heart of God to get me to trust.

the artist

I first met Kent at an exhibition in a famous art gallery. Both of us had been invited to show our work, along with a number of other artists. His paintings were the first things I saw when I came into the gallery: several large, abstract canvasses, hung closely together. They were so dynamic that they immediately drew my attention, and they impressed me as deeply spiritual. As I learned later from talking with Kent, the paintings were his expression of his father's death.

While I was looking at the paintings, Kent approached and introduced himself. He was an art teacher at a nearby university. He was about five feet, nine inches tall, in his early fifties, and immensely strong, with shoulders that were wide and well muscled from weightlifting. There was not an ounce of fat on his body.

I got to know Kent even better after I decided to do graduate work in art, and I saw much more of his work. I learned that he was highly respected by his students, both men and women. It may have been for his strength, though he never flaunted it. It may have been for his ability as an artist. But it was surely also for his integrity, his spirituality. Although he professed no particular religion and was not a "churchgoer," he had a deep sense of the mystery of

43

life and a gift for communicating it to those around him both in conversation and through his art.

Kent was so taken up with his art that often, after teaching a full college load, he would come home to his studio and work all Friday evening, all day Saturday, all day Sunday, and return to the university to teach Monday morning—without sleep!

Everything he created revealed his intense search for contact with the mystery of life: Shamans, Indian holy men riding across the desert, themselves on a search; figures of men holding a rooster about to be immolated; a mother nursing her baby, suffused with light; extraordinary abstracts filled with color and vaguely perceived figures somehow emerging from energetic swirls of paint.

His paintings had the effect of drawing the viewer into a mysterious and unfamiliar landscape, the landscape of the spirit. That is also what I saw when looking into Kent's face, which was extraordinarily sensitive: strength controlled and refined, with eyes that looked in and through. His direct look could be disconcerting.

He often spoke about his father, whom he regarded as an exceptional man. Looking at the artist and the work he had done, I could only imagine what his father must have been like! Kent admired his father and seemed to feel some of that inferiority that a small boy may feel when he sees his father's adult strength and skill. When he spoke about him, I thought back to the great abstract paintings in the gallery.

Once while we were walking, I remarked that his father must have been really great, since Kent, who certainly had that touch of greatness himself, looked up to him. He seemed perplexed for a moment, then said, "My father was a small man, a hunchback, and a cripple. But he never gave up on life." I had the impression that, at one time, his father might have been an embarrassment, and only later did the son, searching, see his true greatness.

When I was invited to Kent's studio, I got a pleasant shock. It was filled not only with paintings but also with huge metal sculptures. Death rode a shiny metal horse—

where God walks

but Death itself was a pregnant women, naked and well-formed, who held in her hands a number of masks, some sorrowful, some grieving, some pleading. Pregnant with what? That was the question a visitor would ask. It was the question I asked myself. Why was she smiling? And why was the piece of art created with black metal?

Moses stood, life-sized, speaking with God from what looked like an inverted metal tent, as though the tent could protect him from his encounter with the Living One.

In all of Kent's art, the drive for the mystical was a predominant force. When I asked him what he experienced while painting, he paused and then said, somewhat hesitantly, "Often times I weep. . . ."

No explanation. No reason, just the fact.

"But why?" I asked.

"Because I am in contact with the mystery."

I wondered if that were possible, and my thoughts were mixed. In one way, I envied him since he could create such beauty that it brought tears to his eyes. I wondered what other people would think if they were told that an artist wept while painting. I even imagined some of the responses in my mind: "That's the way it is with artists, they're so emotional." "Yes, aren't all artists on the edge of madness?"

Was Kent a madman?

Or a prophet?

I thought of the prophets from the scriptures, men and women who had such profound experiences of God that their lives were radically changed. Because of it, they were isolated, set apart. Their choice, it seemed to me, was the same as Kent's: either express what they had experienced, or go mad.

> If I say, "I will not mention [God],
>   or speak any more in his name,"
> then within me there is something like a burning
>   fire
>   shut up in my bones;
> I am weary with holding it in,
>   and I cannot (Jer 20:9).

the bag lady

Sometimes while reading scripture, I get the impression that the events related there took place so long ago, in another country, to another people, that they have little or nothing to do with the world I live in. The stories Jesus told and the life he lived seem so distant, so magical, like beautiful icons hanging on a wall. Pretty, painted myths, hopelessly out of touch with the modern world.

What incredible miracles took place then!

But when I look at my world—the famine in Africa, the many wars throughout the world, the millions of homeless and suffering people—I ask, "Where are the miracles that show Christ's presence now?"

Cynical? Perhaps. Lacking faith? Maybe. I am so conscious of suffering that when it is magnified and reported on a global scale, I guess I expect miracles on that level! Where is God in all this suffering?

Yet scriptures don't say that Jesus healed all the sick and suffering in his country. In fact, he seemed much more involved in healing people one at a time, in real time. I have to constantly remind myself of that.

The newspapers, TV, radio—all these media represent virtual reality, a reality that has been edited and has an agenda. But that is not the reality I live. I do not encounter real people in the media, but simply images on a screen. It's a one-way encounter, a monologue, unlike real life.

I'm usually reminded of this when something happens in my life which makes me look at both scriptures and real life with new eyes. An experience enters into my life, and I get the eerie feeling that I'm seeing it again for the first time. As though it were an icon I had been looking at—then suddenly saw into. There is a difference between looking at and seeing into! It's when I see into, that the events of scripture take on a more profound meaning for me, and the experience that triggers that kind of reaction—and reflection—is always connected with the world I live in here and now, with real people. It has the effect of confronting my lack of faith, with a kind of insighting, a kind of seeing what was not visible before, but hidden and very much at work.

One such experience happened to a friend of mine. When she told me of it, I felt a sense of awe—always a sign of the presence of mystery. I tell the story as I heard it and have thought about it many times since. It's about a bag lady and a woman executive.

The bag lady was in her mid-fifties, bent over with the effort of pushing a shopping cart loaded with personal belongings wrapped in yellow and brown plastic to keep off the rain. She pushed her cart right down the center of a posh shopping mall. She was obviously out of place. People approaching her looked out of the corner of their eye and veered off in another direction. They wanted no part of her. She was poor and dirty; but worse, it was evident that she wanted no sympathy, offered no excuses. There was a toughness about her that offended the better dressed, an inflexibility that repelled them.

Just as she arrived at the glass doors in front of an expensive department store, she paused for a moment and wiped her nose with the sleeve of her dress—if it could be called that, since she seemed to have picked up and put on various articles of clothing, layering them until it was impossible to say what she was wearing. At the very moment she paused, the doors swung open and a woman executive walked out, stunning in well-tailored clothes, clicking importantly on high-heeled shoes. The two women stared at each other. They were from different worlds. The bag lady spat onto the sidewalk and started once more to push her shopping cart when the executive said, "Good afternoon. Can I help you?" She looked down at the woman's feet. The bag lady was wearing only a pair of thongs, no stockings, and she had walked a long way. Her feet were bleeding.

With some surprise and without a word, the bag lady looked the executive up and down. It was clear what she was thinking. As she started to move away, the executive—in a firm, not to be resisted command—said, "Come with me. Come in here." She opened the doors leading into the department store. Surprisingly, the bag lady followed her into the store, past the gaping customers, and into the women's restroom. "Here, sit down," the executive said. And the woman sat down! Then the finely dressed woman said, "Wait here, I'll be right back." In a matter of minutes, she returned, her hands filled with different things. Then she got down on her knees and began to wash the bag lady's feet! She wiped off the blood and the dirt, firmly but gently. She covered the wounds between her toes with cotton and drew on a new pair of rugged stockings.

The bag lady didn't say a word.

Once more the executive told her to stay put, then she went into the store and purchased a pair of soft walking shoes. After putting on the shoes, she washed the woman's hands and face and combed her hair, then led her, speechless, back out onto the sidewalk, where her shopping cart waited. "Can I give you a lift home?" the executive asked. Quite suddenly embarrassment flooded the bag lady's features. Almost roughly—fearful of showing the executive what she called home—the woman said, "No thanks! I can make it on my own." She hesitated, as though weighing whether to say something welling up within her. She looked at the well-dressed woman, and tentatively asked, "Do you think I'm ugly?" The executive, losing her ability to command in the face of such a pathetic question, looked her directly in the eyes and said, "Oh! No."

At that point, the two were no longer in different worlds. They were sharing the same one.

The executive then asked a surprising question: "Tell me, do you believe in God?" The bag lady smiled crookedly, then replied, "Oh, yes, I do. And most especially right now."

I saw something faintly disturbing, even mysterious in this story, as though historical time were suddenly irrelevant, and the events that took place during the life of Jesus were somehow telescoped into the present day and were being reenacted.

I didn't just identify with the story as it had been told 2000 years ago. I was caught right into it! Perhaps time is not linear at all! And perhaps the one whose feet were washed and had oil poured on them, the one who washed the feet of those he loved, what if that one is present—encountering, healing, strengthening?

When things like this happen, I begin to look for the miraculous at the heart of the human encounter; not the external magic, but the inexplicable things that happen when people relate to each other as Christ himself did—I mean, does. When I think this way, I breathe more easily and with more confidence: life is not a tale told by an Idiot full of sound and fury, signifying nothing.

news of a death

I was sitting by a picture window, close to the ocean, watching the hummingbirds streak out of the sky, hover in the air, and sip from the feeder on the outside of the house. I didn't have a care in the world. My eyes wandered from the stacks of wood under the shed to the green vines covering the white picket fence. Everything seemed to shine with the peculiar kind of brilliance characteristic of certain villages close to the ocean.

Lazily, I looked around me. In the process of doing so, I noticed there was a message on the answering machine, so I pressed the button. The message was for me: "I'm sorry to have to break the news this way. . . ." What news? What way? I thought. What is this person talking about? My fear for my family made me leap to conclusions while blocking them out at the same time. I didn't want to hear the rest of the message!

". . . but Father Joe White died on the way to the hospital. It was all so quick. I am sorry you had to hear this on a recording, but I couldn't reach you any other way. I'm sorry."

I sat there, woodenly. I could not believe what I had just heard. What surprised me was my reaction. I was not all that close to the man who had died, at least I hadn't known I was.

I sat for awhile trying to digest the news, vaguely noticing that the weather was changing. It was growing darker and cooler. However, my attention was not on the weather. The injustice of such a sudden death occupied all of my feeling and thinking. I experienced an unreasonable rage. Rising up from within me were questions: Why? Why him? Why now? Why did I care so much?

My emotions were quite mixed, but dominating them all was anger.

I walked out of the house and across the street. A good brisk walk would help me to deal with the anger, and to think.

The weather had changed considerably now, but the change suited my feelings. The sky was storm-black overhead. I walked, head down, praying for the man. Every few steps I interrupted my prayer with expletives. "Damn death! Damn it to hell!" After an outburst, I started to pray again: "Take care of Joe, Lord. He worked hard at serving you. He deserves good treatment"—then, once again, "Damn it all! Damn death. Why does it exist? What's the sense of it?"

I walked for a block or two. Surrounding me were fields of waist-high grass and rustic but expensive homes overlooking and blocking the ocean. I was increasingly aware of the darkness above me. As I turned around to go back home, still praying to God and cursing death, I arrived at a point where I could see, over the fields of grass, the ocean at a distance. My head jerked up. I forgot my prayers and stared. The sky above was a wide band of black, and it was reflected onto the ocean. It lay on the water like a mile-wide swath of black cloth, perfectly matching the color above—but at the limits of the sea, there wasn't a trace of blackness at all! It's as though there were a tent above me that ended one mile out at sea. There the sun shone brilliantly.

I was startled by the contrast.

The horizon, silver and gold, radiant! But right up close, blackness, as impenetrable as the night.

where God walks

Without intending it, I heard within myself: That's death! That is what it's all about. Up close, it makes no sense whatsoever. It's black, obscure, no light at all; but at the horizon line, it becomes transparent, filled with light.

I stood there for some time, aware that this was one of those moments when all of nature is speaking. When that happens, I listen, carefully!

Everything that was happening at that moment was tied into the one awareness: death—and the possibility of something far more mysterious.

I listened in on my inner conversation: "Joe's death, looked at from close-up, is stupid and doesn't make any sense—but out at the horizon, beyond what you see close at hand, what is there?"

I started to walk very slowly, aware that something was working on me.

Turning to my left, I walked through the gates of an old cemetery on top of a hill, hoping to get a better view of the darkness and the sea of silver at the horizon. My mind was very calm now, waiting, but not anxious.

I was no longer praying, nor was I cursing death. I was expectant, listening very closely—for what? I didn't know, but once again my head was lowered, reflecting. Only for a moment did I raise it, when I looked to my left at a gravestone while climbing the small hill. There in large letters was a family name: White.

I'm not sure that it surprised me to see his name there—rather, it seemed like a confirmation of my experience. Everything seemed to fit together at this moment. Joe had passed through the blackness, the shadows, the opaque quality of life, and out through to the silver sea, a whole other dimension. He had passed-over.

It was all right. My anger had disappeared—but not my awareness of the experience. That stayed with me in a surprising way, unconsciously.

After praying, at peace, now, and after writing a letter to some of his friends and mine, I felt reconciled to Joe's death, able to let it go. But in fact, I didn't let it go. It surfaced a month later, in a series of large watercolor landscapes I was working on.

news of a death

I had thought at the time that I was painting land-scapes! In fact, I thought I was being quite objective; but the thing that appealed to me, and which I was trying to capture, was a scene of mountains quite close to the viewer, in the middle of which was an opening, inviting one to pass through to the other side.

As the series of watercolors developed, the opening became more and more severe and defined, the mountains more foreboding. It began to look as though there might not be anything on the other side of the opening! One would then have to go through it without any assurance that it was anything other than a dead end.

With the final painting of the series, a bright gold band began to appear in the opening. At no time did I think I was painting out of the experience I had of Joe's death—not until a friend walked into my studio and said, unexpectedly, "Oh, I see you're dealing with life, death, and the leap of faith."

But of course! I hadn't even known it.

Like all significant things that happen to me, I had to work through Joe's death on both the conscious and unconscious levels; not just in prayer, but, in this case, by painting it out.

The paintings were about that experience by the ocean-side, paintings of anger, helplessness—and faith; paintings of a choice that must be made sooner or later between despair and hope.

The original experience and the paintings came down on the side of hope.

melissa

Melissa is three years old, with an oval shaped face, dark black hair, and chestnut brown eyes. There is only the slightest trace of deviltry in those eyes. Usually they are filled with wonder, since the world is so new. Consequently, it takes only the slightest effort to encourage that wonder to grow: eyes widen, a question lifts her eyebrows just a fraction of an inch—but not a question that demands an answer. It's more like a mysterious sharing, an expectation that the one she is looking at feels the same wonder, and lives in her world. What a delightful surprise to discover that world—even more delightful to actually enter into it. The grown-up in me, so concerned with my self-importance and how to achieve it (what burdens that brings!), can leave everything behind for a moment and enter the world of wonder, a marvelous world, free of reality, free of reason, and full of magic.

One day, Melissa's mother and I were walking and talking on a trail close to the river. Melissa was tagging along, a silent partner. I didn't like that, so when I caught sight of a spot where some rabbits obviously had congregated, I said, "Look at that, Melissa. Do you know what those little round things are?" She stooped to pick one of them up, rolling it between her fingers. Without a word, but with a question in her eyes, she looked at me for the answer. After all, I had raised the question, and this was my opportunity! My invitation, really.

Trying to be confidential and mysterious, I said to her: "Some rabbits have been here. Lots of them. They came here to talk to each other." Such a thing was incomprehensible to her . . . maybe. She knew little more of rabbits other than what she had seen in children's books. That they could actually talk to one another was what surprised and intrigued her.

Since I knew that rabbits often crossed the path on which we were walking, I tried my luck and said, "Do you want me to call to some rabbits so you can see them?" "Yes," she said. "Oh! I'd like that!" With feigned assurance—I was working on the odds that a rabbit would have to cross our path sooner or later—I whistled three times. She looked to the left, then to the right. No rabbits. For a while we had been engaged in a game of magic, but since the rabbits were not complying, I stepped out of her world of wonder and started talking again with her mother.

While talking (my mind was still on Melissa), I thought I heard the hoot of an owl from the other side of the river, and I was sure that Melissa had not. I was determined to try once more to enter into her world. After some reflection, I realize this says a great deal about my own need!

I bent down to her level and said, "There are great birds that live in these trees and we can talk with them, did you know that?" Even as I spoke the words, I imagined the great birds in the trees, waiting for an invitation. So was Melissa! In fact, so was I!

Still bending down, I imitated the sound of an owl, aiming my voice at the other side of the water. There was no response. It was a one-way conversation! Melissa gave me that questioning look once more. Again I made the sound of an owl. No answer, but just as we were about to continue our walk, three hoots from an owl floated back across the river. Melissa looked in that direction, then quickly at me, thinking perhaps that I was making the sound. When she saw that I wasn't, her face registered the question she

60

must have been asking: Can a person really talk to birds? But of course! Again I made the owl sound, and again the owl answered from across the water. It was pure magic, a world both of us had entered together.

I had no idea how long I could keep this up, but once more I made the owl sound, and once more there was a response. Melissa lost all capacity for words. I whispered in the most conspiratorial way: "Try it, Melissa, try to talk to the owl. Do it and the owl will talk back to you." A little uncertainly she attempted a high pitched sound. Lucky for me, the owl hooted once more. Melissa was now certain that I was a magician, and so was she!

With the apparent success of talking with an owl to my credit, I decided on greater things. I knew that the path we were walking would soon terminate near a pond in and around which were ducks and geese, so I asked Melissa if I should whistle for a great white bird to come. She looked up and said, "Oh yes, tell the bird to come. A white one, a big one!"

Once more I whistled. Nothing happened. After a few seconds, Melissa asked, "Where is the white bird? I don't see him." "The bird will be just around the corner by a lake," I said, "you'll see." Meanwhile I said to myself, "I can't go wrong on this one since there are always birds around that pond, and always at least one or two are white." I didn't want the magic to end. The world of wonder and magic is fragile.

As we came to the end of the path and the beginning of the pond, I looked, and there on the far bank was a white goose—not very impressive in size, but at least it was white! "See, Melissa, there's the white bird right over there. Do you see it?" "No, I don't. Where?" With some difficulty I got her to focus her attention on the far bank where the bird was, but I could tell that she was losing faith. The bird was not very impressive. But then, all of a sudden, a really great white bird flew in from over the river, a magnificent creature with a tremendous wing span. It was easily the largest bird in the area. Majestically it soared over our heads and flew to the top of the highest tree, landing there.

Melissa was wide eyed, eyebrows all the way up! So was I! The worlds of wonder and reality were merging!

The bird was so magnificent and could be seen so easily that we sat down on the grass and watched it. It turned its head proudly from the left to the right as though surveying everything below it. I told Melissa that this was the king of the birds. She believed every bit of it—just as she believed in my ability to talk to the animals.

We were both in the world of the child, where belief comes so easily. In that world, there is nothing so unusual that it can't be believed. There are no child-atheists, for children don't know what cynicism is yet.

Not wanting to press my luck, but also unwilling to disengage myself from this special moment, I noticed that the bird was beginning to stretch its neck. I thought to myself, it will soon fly away. So, I turned to Melissa and asked her, "Do you want me to send the great bird back across the river? Shall I tell it to go home where it belongs?" "Yes," she said, "do that." Once again taking a chance, I whistled two times. No sooner had I whistled than the bird, for its own reasons, lifted its wings and flew back across the river. My reputation was assured. But how did the bird know?

As we walked away from the pond, dark-haired Melissa looked up to me and said, "Can I put my hand in yours? I like you. Will you teach me how to talk to the animals?"

As though I could! The very question reveals that undeniable quality that we admire in children, their trust, their belief in the adult world. Theirs is the ability—the need!—to give themselves to adults, to believe in what they say. When an adult encounters that trust from a child, it usually triggers a corresponding, protective attitude in him or her, a kind of sacred trust then springs up between the child and the adult, a trust in which everything is possible.

Certainly there is a protective shell that envelops a child. It holds in a world of magic and wonder, and because of this, belief in God comes quite naturally. It is rare to meet a cynical child! Still, that childlike wonder and humor is not restricted to children. Every so often one encounters it in an adult, as I did in Aunt Mary.

aunt mary

Certain special people have come into my life and moved me deeply. Whenever this happens, something is ignited; I catch a glimpse of what life is really about. My grim predictions of the future vanish; so, too, do the pretentious ideas in my head, put there by my need to control life and make it predictable. The scientist in me surrenders to the poet, and I see something of the Mystery at work. This is what happened in my friendship with Aunt Mary Frost.

A Sister of Mercy first told me about her. "Father, you should meet Aunt Mary. She is such a good person—and wise. You would be surprised at the things she says. Perhaps you could bring her communion?"

I was purposefully vague in my reply. "Yes, perhaps sometime." However, the sister was not going to be put off. A few days later she asked me if I would take communion to Aunt Mary that very day. I fumbled around a bit and came up with, "Oh, yes of course." But I volunteered with reluctance, since I had a lot of desk work to get out of the way. My agenda!

That day, I was driven to a one-story, rough-board house outside the modest city of Auburn, California. Before we got out of the car, a small, mean looking dog, named Bo, let us know we were not welcome. I went into the house cautiously, with the Sister of Mercy leading the way, talking down the dog.

Aunt Mary was sitting up in a bed covered with a bright-colored quilt, waiting. Her white hair framed a face wrinkled with years of living. When we entered her room, she looked in our direction, responding to the noise—not to what she could see, for she was blind.

A radio was propped up on her bed against the rough lumber wall. Next to it was a telephone. Behind her hung a large cincture rosary, the kind the sisters used to wear around their waists. Her bed was parallel to a wood stove, on top of which simmered a tin cup of tea. The house had a good, warm, lived-in feeling.

When I was introduced to Aunt Mary, she simply nodded, barely acknowledging my presence—nothing rude, just aloof: she didn't know me. Only after prayer and communion did she talk. And what a surprise—she had plenty to say!

I learned that Mary was born around the year 1885, a Nomlaki Indian, in the town of Red Bluff, California. When Mary was two years old, her mother died and she went to live with the Sisters of Mercy in an orphanage until she was seven. From there she moved to a city hospital.

"What were you doing there?" I asked.

"Livin' with a bunch of old ladies. I was always pickin' on those old women because they was so cranky. So I used to catch toads and put them in their beds. It scared them half to death."

Aunt Mary hesitated, then attempted an explanation. "Most of the time I try to be good. Other times I try to be as mean as possible. Misery loves company." Then with a half-smile that came from knowing first-hand what old women have to put up with, she confessed: "I don't know what I'd do now if someone put toads in my bed!"

At sixteen Mary met Ben Frost, also an Native American. They married and traveled together throughout Northern California and Nevada, wherever the jobs were, or whenever they got bored with living too long in one place.

"I so loved the horses!" she said. "And Tehama county was beautiful, the fields and the hills. Those were good days. We just picked up and went whenever we felt like it. Ben could do anything and I went right along with him—even when he went into a boat. And I don't swim. I've always been scared of the water, but I trusted Ben."

A few years before I met Mary Frost, Ben, her husband, died. Then Mary had a stroke, which crippled her. Her biggest disappointment was that she could no longer ride horses.

Once confined to bed, much of Aunt Mary's time was spent in silence. I asked her about this, if she found the time heavy and hard to endure. I asked because I think I would have found it unbearable, as though my life had ended and there were nothing more to do but to wait for death.

Aunt Mary thought about the question for awhile, then turned her head and looked at me out of half-closed eyes, as though she could see my face. "Well, sometimes I talk to myself. People say, 'How come you're talking to yourself?' I tell them I want to talk to someone who has some knowledge. Sometimes I talk to Bo, my dog. And sometimes I sing. Bo leaves. He doesn't like my singing."

The woman would not be depressed! She made sickness, immobility, and the imminent presence of death lifesize. I could see before me someone who was calm in the face of what was still dreadful to me.

Mary thought a lot about the past, but offered some keen observations about the present, especially about nuclear weapons and the race for arms. "People are gettin' too smart, each country tryin' to outdo the other. Tryin' to play God and can't do it. He'll let them get so far, then he'll stop them."

Wisdom is reserved for those who struggle through the passages of life, accepting each one of them, while still remaining open to the future. Although chronologically old, Aunt Mary's spirit was as young and vigorous as Melissa's. She was a wise woman.

Several years ago, in the month of October, Aunt Mary celebrated her one-hundredth birthday at a party with her family and friends. Her house was filled with those who loved her. After the celebration had quieted down she confided to me: "Well, I'm not quite a hundred, but it's good to have a party just the same. They enjoyed it and so did I."

Later, when someone told her she was beautiful, she coolly ignored the remark, was silent a bit, then said, as though introducing a new topic of conversation, "You know, beauty is skin deep. Character is what you look at."

For a period of four years I visited and came to know Aunt Mary—not that we ever grew "chummy." That wasn't her way. But we did become friends. I asked her once what it felt like to reach advanced old age. She digested my question, but said nothing. I waited, staring at the tea simmering on the stove. Somewhere from beneath the bed, Bo scratched himself and the floor at the same time. I began to think that Aunt Mary hadn't heard me, or didn't intend to answer. But she had heard.

"It's good that people don't know when they're going. I'd go quicker then, because I was worried. I think we know too much anyway—or think we do."

She paused, then grew silent again, for what seemed a long time. I studied her features, especially the character lines that creased her face. I wondered at the experiences that had formed them. Aunt Mary seemed to be looking at the ceiling, though her eyes were closed. She opened them partially. "The way everything happens is for the best," she said. "I wonder, though. Someone must watch over you and guide you along your way."

Her interests centered on her family, her friends, God, the Dodgers, and her dreams. "You know, I used to dream a lot, then I stopped. But a few nights ago I woke up from a deep sleep and saw a vision. There were four horses standing there. What do you think that vision means?"

I hesitated. The four horsemen in scripture signify impending judgment. I had no intention of suggesting such a thing to Aunt Mary, so I tried an evasion: "In the Bible the four horsemen signify an end of one thing and the beginning of something else." What I said was true enough, but I was hedging. Then an idea occurred to me, so I asked her, "Were there men on the horses?"

"No. There were no men. Just the horses standing there at the foot of the bed." Relieved, and more assured, I asked, "Did the vision make you feel good?"

"It sure did!" she replied. "I felt fine."

"Well, Aunt Mary," I suggested, "the next time you get a vision and you don't like it, just tell the vision, 'I don't accept you.' And when you get one you do like, you can tell that one, 'I accept you.'"

"OK," Aunt Mary said, "I'll just do that."

And I believe she did.

A month later, with her usual good humor and calmness, she arranged her funeral: who was to be invited ("You've got to tell those Indians you want them to come or they won't come"), where it was to be, who was to speak. She was surprisingly alert on her last day. I felt that she consented to her death; it didn't catch her unawares. And she brought the same sense of presence to her dying that she had to her living.

On an overcast day in November, with intermittent showers, the body of Aunt Mary Frost was lowered into the earth. As for Aunt Mary herself? She was set free at last, maybe even to be with her beloved horses! No plot of ground could contain such a wise spirit.

the directed retreat

A sister, who was a teacher, was in the fourth day of an eight-day retreat, and it was her assigned time to see the retreat director to talk over her inner life.

I was the director.

She entered the room like a walking stick, thin, old, and austere, looking as though she were being pinched from within by some force that wrinkled her features once and for all. I wasn't sure what to expect.

Rather stiffly she sat opposite me and began to talk. "I have to get ready to die. I recently had a stroke."

I thought, Well, that's getting right to the point in a hurry.

Then the sister began to tell me what was wrong with all the people in her department at school: So-and-so didn't use her head, and forgot to make out her reports. Someone else didn't even have the ability to teach the subject assigned. A third was too unstable; a fourth didn't turn in her grades at the proper time.

It was obvious she thought she was surrounded by incompetent people, including the superior of her community, who didn't trust her—at least this is what she thought and felt. Still, I wondered what her nervous complaints had to do with her opening statement: "I have to get ready to die."

Perhaps, I thought, she is worried about who will take over the department after she is gone, as though she were indispensable. Maybe.

Fumbling around for a starting place, something to say, I suggested: "I guess you have to be patient, don't you? You can't get a perfect world, and frequently people don't measure up to your expectations. When they fail, you get angry." This was a safe thing to say, I thought. But within I was thinking: she's afraid of dying. How does it show up in her thought? "No one can replace me. They are all incompetent."

But the sister was not tuned in to what I was thinking. She had her own agenda and was slowly working it out.

She fidgeted a bit, moving around in her chair as though she were grinding something beneath her—or within her! Then, quite unexpectedly, she changed the direction of the conversation: "You know, I tried to make a directed retreat last year, the first one in my life. Each day I went to see the young priest-director and we talked. But I got nothing out of it, and he was getting more and more frustrated. Finally he told me, 'Sister, I can't help you. I have no idea what to say to you or what to suggest. I think you had better go to someone else. I am incapable of directing you during this retreat.'"

I identified with the previous director!

"Well," she said, "I got up and walked out. And he was a Jesuit, too; he is supposed to know something about retreats and direction! I was so mad that I walked out to the parking lot and just stood there, looking down at the ground."

She continued talking, "My retreat was over! And it was a failure. Then I thought I heard something, like the wind. I looked up at the sky, but there was nothing. It was within me. I remember I felt quite light. And the wind said, with great clarity and assurance: 'I have already forgiven you, why don't you forgive the others?'"

It was in the telling of the story of her first directed retreat—which she thought was a complete failure—that she suddenly realized the connection between the

where God walks

experience she had then and her complaints about all of the people around her. It was a sharp moment of awareness.

She had been forgiven. Why wasn't she passing that same forgiveness on to others?

She sat bolt upright in her chair and stopped grinding whatever it was within her. Her eyes opened wide with the realization of the grace she had received out on the parking lot, and how she was supposed to make use of it in preparing for her death.

She had been forgiven, she was certain of that. Then the question: Why not forgive the others, the others she was surrounded by, the incompetent ones in her department, in her community? Her superior?

This was the preparation for death she had been talking about.

In that moment of grace, she saw. It was not that she was afraid of death, rather, there was still something to be done, and she might not have enough time to do it! And she wanted to do it.

At that moment, she knew with certainty that the most important thing—and the most difficult—was to forgive.

It was a moment of grace.

the encounter

Søren Kierkegaard, the nineteenth-century philosopher and religious writer, said that it is sometimes possible to get a hint of what our own personal story is by looking backward, but that it must be lived going forward. This rings true for me, especially when looking at encounters and friendships that have deeply affected my life. Think for a moment of a few of your close friends. Did you choose that friend? Or did your paths somehow cross, almost accidentally?

There seems to be a grid just below the surface of our lives, and where the lines intersect, that is where the encounter can take place. But it is only after the encounter that we consciously and freely choose the friendship. Looking back, it seems as though it had to exist. There is a necessity about it, despite the fact that it was freely chosen.

The grid is a spatial image for something far more mysterious, the Grid-maker, the power or force—call it what you like—that seems to bring people together in a deeply significant way.

Paul in his letter to the Philippians has no doubt as to who the Grid-maker is:

> I thank my God every time I remember you, constantly praying with joy in every one of my prayers

for all of you, because of your sharing in the gospel from the first day until now. I am confident of this, that the one who began a good work among you will bring it to completion by the day of Jesus Christ. It is right for me to think this way about all of you, because you hold me in your heart, for all of you share in God's grace with me. . . . For God is my witness, how I long for all of you with the compassion of Christ Jesus (Phil 1:3-8).

There always remains a mystery about a friendship or an encounter, one which can never fully be cleared up. The truth of this came home to me with quite a shock because of a young girl I met in an art class some years ago.

On the first day of the class, the students were arranging their materials, getting ready to paint. I looked around at them—every age and description, and all of them strangers. I had never seen any of them before.

Nevertheless, one girl in particular stood out clearly. She had dark hair and seemed very quiet, something of an introvert. I have no idea what made me focus on her rather than someone else in the class, but I did.

A week or two went by with nothing more than an occasional thought about her, but it was an unusual thought: that I would have something to do with her. I dismissed the thought from my mind.

One day while leaving the class, I looked down at her desk to see what she was painting. I was so surprised that I stopped and stared at the picture. In it two people caught up in the air were communicating. One was slightly higher than the other—but these "people" were not representational. They had the exterior shapes of people, but without faces; in fact, they had no identifying marks at all. They were composed of colorful, luminous dots of paint. Some common energy force seemed to make up their faces and bodies, as well as the background of the picture. It flowed between them, in them, as though a superior form of communication were taking place, non-audible, but direct.

where God walks

I stopped and stared. This is not the usual kind of painting one would expect to see in a watercolor class. I looked at the painting, then at the girl. She had depth. It was obvious in the painting. My first impression proved right.

In her painting, she was dealing with the mystery of encounter and relationship. I learned later that she had just spent seven months in a Hindu ashram, a place of study and prayer. She was twenty-three years old.

From that time on we got to know one another, perhaps because of a common interest in art—that certainly was part of it. More significantly, the beginning of the friendship had something to do with the subject of the painting she was working on: an encounter with another force working in and through both of us, the Grid-maker.

Once the lines below the surface crossed, we made a conscious decision.

We took long walks together, and our conversation had a wide range of interests, all of them centered on the inner life of art, creativity, and above all, the ever-mysterious Spirit. There were inner landscapes to explore just as interesting as the landscapes we walked through—and sometimes just as dangerous.

Some inner landscapes can never be shared. They are too profound. But those we could share, we did.

One evening we got into a discussion about Jesus Christ, and I asked her what she thought about him. "He was a good man."

"Is that all?" I asked. "He claimed—and people believe—that he is the Son of God." I was trying to make a convert.

"Well," she answered, "whether he is or isn't, what difference does it make?"

My ego was somewhat deflated, but I returned to the attack. "I think it makes a lot of difference, since if he is God and man, then he is present to you, now, as God and man—which says a lot about being human. Christ rejects nothing genuinely human. That's the difference it makes."

The conversation ended as such conversations do, in mutual disappointment. No one is argued into believing.

Before parting, I got a promise out of her to try reading the Gospel of Saint John. I was still trying to make a convert! I had the naive idea that the only thing necessary to come to the truth was to pick up the scriptures and read them.

She kept her promise, then returned the book and told me, "I got nothing out of this book."

I felt a sense of defeat, then I thought to myself, Well she has a mystical bent, perhaps something more abstract would appeal to her. I gave her the first letter of John to read. She read it, and returned it with the same comment, so I gave up on giving her anything to read.

A few months later, I finished the work I was doing at the university we were both attending. It was time to say good-bye. Despite our disagreements about Christ and scripture, we had had some good walks, talks, and meals together. We had become friends almost without knowing it.

Just before leaving, I was doing a painting in my studio. She had come to say good-bye and while there, asked me, "What is the purpose of forming relationships in life? They end so quickly. What meaning do they have?"

I didn't realize that she was feeling the coming separation keenly. We had, over the space of four months, been able to share a lot. Many of the questions she had asked herself from early childhood found some answers because of it; and I myself had learned to see art differently because of the way she looked at life. She was thinking, I believe, that something good would now end.

I tried to answer her question (somewhat naively, looking back) by saying something about friendships being given to us to get an idea of what life is really about. "That is why I gave you the scriptures. I had hoped that you would get some idea of what life was about in reading them."

"I get much more from talking with you than I do from reading. And I learn more too."

I thought a lot about that remark over the next few days, turning it over in my mind and my feelings. It was my turn, now, to feel disappointed, not because of the

where God walks

separation, though I felt that also, but rather because I thought she was saying she preferred my company and conversation to Christ's. Perhaps this sounds dense, but I was determined that she should discover Christ—and by reading a book!

I was ignoring the primary way Mystery speaks to us: through others. That is when the light kindled in my brain. Of course! That's it! Christ didn't hand his disciples a book and tell them to read all about him. He spoke with them, shared their fears and their hopes, their feelings. He spent time walking with them, enjoyed their company, broke bread with them—and that is when they saw him! In the breaking of the bread.

Armed with my new insight which confirmed what she had said earlier, I set up a luncheon meeting just before a class we both attended. I wanted to tell her she was right after all.

To prepare for the luncheon, I typed out the whole story of the disciples on the road to Emmaus, and put it, folded, on the back of an icon of the three visitors to Abraham, a famous work of art by the Russian artist Rublev. The early Christians saw the meeting of the three visitors with Abraham as a sign of the Trinity and the eucharist. The reproduction, which was quite a nice one, was my parting gift.

We met outside of the student union building of the university. I greeted her with, "You know, you're right after all. I didn't see what you were driving at when we were talking about relationships in my studio, but I do now."

She looked tired. Her head was hanging. She gave me a warning glance and said, "My head is hurting. I would prefer not to get into anything very heavy."

I paid no attention to the clear hint. I was going to tell her all about the two disciples on the road to Emmaus and how they met Christ! And it wasn't through a book. I wanted to say to her, "You were right. We understand much more about the Mystery from giving and receiving, from friendship, than from reading books."

Seated at the table, I started telling her the story. Her head hung lower. I ignored it, and her too, in a way. Finally, oblivious to everything around me, I got to the point in the story where Christ explains the meaning of the scriptures to the two dejected disciples. Then, magnanimously, I said, "You were right. He didn't give them a book to read. It was a living thing between him and them. They got more out of his conversation than they would have out of reading the scriptures. You were right all along."

No reaction. The head still hung low.

Not noticing the danger signals, or not wanting to, I continued the story, telling her how they asked him into their home, and sat down to eat. At this part of the story, I took a piece of bread in my hands and said (without really thinking about the connection with the story I was telling—I was just hungry!) Christ took the bread, then blessed it, and the disciples suddenly realized who it was that was eating with them. They saw the Lord in the breaking of the bread.

I paused. Her head snapped up.

She was looking directly at me with eyes one hundred percent focused. There was an intensity in that expression which disarmed me, so much so that I stopped telling the story, with the sure conviction that she not only had a headache, but was angry. That kind of look I have seen only on people who were intensely angry or recovering from brain surgery! It was as though she were fixing in her mind and imagination every particular of my face and features. As though she had to!

I quickly ended the story, stumbling around a bit. I interpreted her look as extreme dissatisfaction.

One more time before I left the university, we had the chance to take a long walk, ending up in a restaurant. Sitting opposite me, she said, "I'd like to explain something to you about the way I believe."

"All right, go ahead."

"There may be a world outside of this restaurant," she said, "but I don't live in that world. I live right here, in this booth. In this present moment. I hope there is a world outside, but I'm not living there. I'm living here. Do you understand what I mean?"

where God walks

I didn't have the faintest idea of what she meant, though I did agree with living in the present moment. A bit skeptically I said, "OK. So you're not living there but here. But don't you really think there is a world outside the doors of the restaurant?"

"No, I don't. I'm not living there. I am living right here, at this moment."

"Uh huh. . . ."

"Do you remember when you gave me the gospel of John to read?

"Yes, I do," I answered.

"Well, I didn't live in that gospel. Nor did I live in the letter of John either."

I had no idea where she was going, or even that this was an important conversation. I attributed what she was saying to her unique way of seeing. Artists are different, and they see differently.

"You mean you didn't get much out of either one?"

"No, I don't mean that. I mean that I didn't live in them."

"Oh . . . ?"

"But remember when you were telling me about the disciples on the road, how they met . . . er,"—and this came out almost painfully—"him? Do you remember how they recognized who he was, in the breaking of the bread?"

"Yes, I do."

"Well, I lived in that."

There was a long pause on my part. It was my turn now to get one hundred percent focused. At last I saw what she was talking about.

"Are you saying that you believe that Christ is in the breaking of the bread?"

My mind took off on a flight of its own. I couldn't believe what she was saying: the very same thing that I was recounting was taking place in her—in the act of breaking the bread!

"Yes," she said, slowly, "I do believe that . . . that he . . . he is in the breaking of the bread."

For a week following this conversation, I had to deliberately distract myself from thinking about it. This ancient story about the disciples, which was told originally as a way of teaching Christians how they encounter Christ, in the stranger, in the word shared, in the breaking of the bread—suddenly it was all present, contemporary. It had actually taken place!

Two strangers had met, shared the word together, broken bread—and the Mystery stood in our midst! Not coming from the outside either, but from within.

Once more time had collapsed. The scriptural icon was no longer a dead word on a page two thousand years old but a living event in which we both found ourselves, along with the one who stands center to all relationships.

Rembrandt captured something of the surprise in such an encounter. His painting of the meal in Emmaus depicts the very moment when two discouraged disciples discover who their friend is. Jesus sits bolt upright, his hands in his lap, his head almost touching the wall in back of him, composed, kingly. One of the two disciples sits facing him, to his right. He stares in disbelief, his left arm on the table. He is leaning to his right, almost off balance. His right arm seems to hang to the floor. The shock of realization approaches terror—perhaps awe would be the better word, a mixture of fear and disbelief.

The table the two are sitting at seems to be pushed into a corner of the room and from that corner a bright light glows—no ordinary light either, but the light that God created on the first day of creation. The disciple is looking upon a new creation, Christ resurrected. He is simply stunned. Off to the left and in the background of the painting, the other disciple is rushing from the room, perhaps on his way back to Jerusalem. He, too, is surrounded by the same light of recognition and disbelief.

At the very moment of the breaking of the bread, the underlying grid became visible to the two disciples. They saw the interconnectedness.

In that moment, they chose what God had brought about, a friend.

82   where God walks

the invisible man

On the streets were many of the people who work for the state, all dressed quite handsomely in suits and ties. The women walked briskly, chatting with one another, the sound of high heels clicking on the pavement. It was the kind of cool, sunny, autumn day when it feels good to be alive. There was an electricity in the air, as though great things were being accomplished, or were about to be! Most of the "down and outers," the poor, usually avoid this part of the city. Police on horses patrol the well-tended park surrounding the California State Capitol building, keeping order and making certain the benches are not used as beds.

As I approached the light to cross the street, I saw out of the corner of my eye a man standing about twenty feet to my right. I knew instinctively that the man was homeless. With an instant dislike, I turned to the left, away from the man, and started walking a few steps. As I did, a thought rushed into my mind: the man looked like my father! He looked about the same age, but was dressed in a long, shabby coat, and was unsteady on his feet.

He was probably wondering whether he could make it across the street, even though he had the light in his favor. He was an old man, after all.

I stopped, with the image of my father sharply etched in my mind. Then I looked back in his direction. Was I too

85

proud to ask the man if he needed help crossing the street? I asked myself. No, I decided with some reluctance, I wasn't.

As I turned toward him, I could see the well-dressed people coming toward me on the street. They could see me, too—right up to the time I got close to the old man and asked him if he needed help. At that precise moment, I became invisible.

It was an uncanny experience! I had been visible, I was sure. But the moment I touched the old man, both of us became invisible. People walked right on by without seeing us. Even as we crossed the street—the only ones to cross the intersection at that time—we were not seen. I felt uneasy.

On the other side of the street, a television crew was climbing all over their equipment, moving and angling for the best shots of the Capitol building. They were getting ready for some important event about to happen. Still, not one person looked at us, so easily had we slipped into another dimension of existence.

Once on the other side of the street, I asked the old man where he was going. In a kind of resigned voice, filled with great fatigue, he told me he had a friend who lived a few blocks away. His friend would give him a place to stay for the night.

I asked him if he needed any money, and what he would do with it if he got it. "I'd buy some food, that's what I'd do with it."

"You're sure you wouldn't drink it up?"

"Nope, I wouldn't. I used to, but it ruined my health. Those days are finished. Can't take it anymore."

All during the time that we were talking, people passed us by, not noticing us, even though the old man had slid down the pole he was resting against and half sat on the pavement—he wasn't drunk.

"Well," I said, "wait here and I'll get you some money. I have about twenty bucks on me, but I need ten myself. You can have the other ten if you wait here."

"OK, I'll wait." I didn't think he would.

where God walks

I left him and walked up the Capitol steps to get change. Once I left the old man, propped against the light pole, I noticed that people could see me again. I even had a good but brief conversation with the lady who made the change, real eyeball to eyeball contact! We were in the same world.

With ten dollars in my wallet and ten in my hand, I went back out on the street where the old man waited. He was in the same position, half sitting, half leaning against the pole.

"Here you go," I said. "Here's ten dollars. Promise you won't drink it away?"

"I can promise that. I'll get food with it."

I helped him get to his feet. He stood there unsteadily, turned and started to walk toward his friend's house, wherever that was. Then I turned away and started back to my car.

And once again, I became visible!

People made eye contact with me now, even nodding hello. I was part of the real world once more! I felt relieved. I could breathe more freely. The old man continued down the street in back of me, still invisible.

The incident left me feeling good but somewhat disturbed; after all, my first reaction had been to turn away. At first, I didn't want to see the old man. I actually turned away from seeing him. I wanted him not to be there, to be invisible, in fact.

It was that twinge of guilt that made me turn back toward him. He looked like my father—and that made him visible. I could see what I did not want to see, but what was there.

saint ives

Saint Ives is a small village perched on the southwest point of England in the province of Cornwall. The people who live there are fiercely proud of their heritage and of their language, which is intimately connected with the surrounding sea on which they depend for their living.

A great wall surrounds the city where it meets the sea. The wall is protection for the port, which is filled with fishing boats. From the shore the village rises up steeply as though carved out of stone. Everything in Saint Ives seems made out of stone: the harbor wall, the buildings, the streets, the landscapes, even the people, with their toughened skin and lined faces.

People have lived in Saint Ives since before the time of Christ. Their relics are still visible, giving the land a sense of mystery. Boulders three times the size of a person stand isolated in fields overlooking the sea. There is an Easter-Island feeling about these rocks. And from the air one can see great round circles of stone, just below the surface of the land, that were once ancient religious sites and meeting places.

The village centers itself around the harbor and the business of fishing. When the tide is in, the boats proudly ride the surface of the sea. When out, the boats are ungraciously strewn on the sand, somewhat desolately, resembling the aftermath of a war that has been fought and lost.

I got to know Saint Ives quite well when I spent a month there painting. I had joined a class which I had heard was excellent. It wasn't, so I excused myself from attending, and went out on my own to paint rather than remaining in a closed, crowded studio. As a result, I walked all over the village getting the feel of the place. I even got to know some of the residents.

The sound of the surf was constantly in my ears, as well as the loud, raucous screams that came from the biggest sea gulls I had ever seen. They were gigantic, snow white, and they covered the sky at times, always on the lookout for food. The gulls of Saint Ives are not only bigger but also bolder than their American counterparts. They fought each other viciously for a scrap of food, even though they were all well fed.

One day I walked to the top of the village to look out over the sea. The narrow streets in Saint Ives were made not for automobiles, but for people; and, like everything in the village, they were made to resist the sea, the severe winters, and the howling winds that come sweeping across this small peninsula.

I had climbed upward for some time when, all at once, I came out onto a meeting of four streets overlooking the harbor. The view was stunning. Just as I was about to enter the juncture of the four streets, I caught sight of a great gull, directly in front of me, on the opposite side of the street. It was walking slowly toward me without seeing me. One wing was broken and the bird seemed confused. Across its snow-white breast was a splash of brilliant red blood.

Once it saw me, the bird hesitated. It didn't seem to know which way to turn. It started to move to the right, but some people were coming up the hill from that side; then it turned to the left, saw me again, and hesitated, even more

where God walks

confused. It wandered around a little, then reversed itself, and dragging its broken wing went back the way it had come.

The whole experience rooted me to the spot, it was so unexpected and dramatic: the broken wing, the brilliant red against the white, the confusion and helplessness. All thought vanished from my mind. It was a moment of experience, a moment of intent listening. For what, I didn't know. I supposed I expected the bird would die, unable to fly and compete for food. Why the incident registered so firmly in my mind, I did not understand at the time.

I turned to the left and started down the hill and across the village, on my way to find a church. Little by little the incident dropped out of my awareness as I met people and was caught up in the busyness of the village. There were many tourists, and a kind of holiday atmosphere prevailed.

On the opposite side of the village, at the top of a hill, stood the church I was looking for, but the friend I was expecting to meet had not yet arrived. Reluctantly, I sat down to wait, but I grew steadily more impatient. He was late, and I did not want to be there.

My impatience turned to fidgeting. To distract myself, I started looking around at the inside of the church. It was anything but lovely. The nave of the narrow, bony structure was crowded with pews, and garish pictures, not at all to my taste, covered the walls. But my eyes kept coming back to a particularly ugly crucifix, done in gaudy colors, which hung above the main altar. It showed Jesus in agony, looking up to the heavens.

It was not a well made crucifix, and it was obvious that the body had come from a badly conceived mold. I turned away in disgust, looking at the cheap, imitation stain-glass windows instead. Then my eyes returned again to the gaudy crucifix! Abruptly, unexpectedly, the image of the wounded sea gull forced its way into my consciousness. It seemed as though the two images somehow fused together: the gaudy image of the figure of Christ on the cross, and the brilliant white sea gull stained blood red, confused and not knowing which way to turn.

I looked more closely at the figure on the cross, stretched hand and foot, nailed and pierced in the side, dazed, in shock, not comprehending what was happening. All roads blocked, no escape—like the gull!

And the Man on the hill!

I had a very clear awareness that something was broken on top of that hill, grief-stricken and confused, not knowing which way to turn.

I saw the image of that breaking all around me. I was no longer restless or impatient as I thought: Christ is no stranger to violence, or to suffering and pain.

The sea gull was a reminder, a wrenching of the heart.

guidance

I have often opened the Bible looking for a passage that would give me assurance that God was with me. And sometimes I have come across a passage that has helped me, especially when I have been feeling alone or too full of myself to get perspective. When I read something like, "Do not fear, for I am with you, do not be afraid, for I am your God; I will strengthen you, I will help you, I will uphold you" (Is 41:10), I feel a sense of relief that everything doesn't depend on me.

I am also reassured by this passage: "For I, the Lord your God, hold your right hand; it is I who say to you, 'Do not fear, I will help you'" (Is 41:13).

When I really listen to these words and pray over them, I cease being an all-important adult for awhile and remember that I am a child holding the hand of a Father who cares for me.

Of course, all of this depends on my being able to listen. And I don't always listen.

If I get caught up in my own needs, if I am willing to sacrifice other people's needs to my own, I stop listening. I go deaf! I get caught in a trap that ego springs, either out of fear or desire. Then, loaded down with self-importance or wounded pride, I question God's guidance. I begin to wonder if he is even interested.

In other words, I forget.

I have discovered that when I really forget, I need more than just a thought to recall me to my senses. I need an earthquake—something that shakes me up and opens me to my deepest self. Earthquakes have a way of rearranging the landscape.

Some years ago I was attending a religious congress, but only halfheartedly. I had no real interest in the speakers, or the crowds. The things for sale weighed me down with boredom. But I did look forward to meeting a good friend while there. That's why I had come.

Unfortunately, after meeting and talking, we got into a serious disagreement. It left both of us with hurt feelings and wounded pride. At the end of the congress, we went our separate ways.

I was smoldering. Worse, I had a deep sense of guilt about my part in causing the argument. Feeling estranged and alienated, I was certain I had lost a valuable friend.

While involved in the unending negative internal dialogue that so often follows a perceived failure, I met up with a priest friend I had not seen for several months. We started walking and talking together.

The beginning of the conversation was general enough, but little by little I began to recount my experience of failure, my negative mood—even my anger at the priesthood, the church, and the world—and, especially, my reservations about all authority! Everything was swept up into my angry mood.

All of this took place at a time when priests and sisters were leaving the religious life like the last of autumn's leaves in a brisk wind. Some people even thought the wind was the Holy Spirit. It was a period of great unrest, which offered fuel for the fire of my anger.

My friend tried to persuade me that my feelings were part of a growth process and that God was somehow involved. Sure, I thought. The more he tried to talk sense into me, the more angry I became, until finally I said, "I

where God walks

really don't care about the church. It can make it on its own. Nor do I feel I owe any obligation to my fellow priests. In fact, I could easily leave!"

My friend was shocked—so was I! Words were pouring out of my mouth that I had never allowed into my conscious mind.

"You can't do that," my friend said. "You've put too many years into it. What about your promises? You can't just throw something like that over. It's not that easy!"

Stung by his opposition, I became even more vehement—not unlike Peter in the midst of his betrayal—"The hell I can't!" With that, I turned and walked away, carrying my prayer book with me.

Once I was alone, I nursed my frustration and self-pity. At least there was no one in sight, no one to put on a show for, no one to contradict me.

Quite incongruously, considering how adamant I had been about leaving everything behind, the thought came to my mind that I should read my prayer book, which I had neglected to do that day.

Opening the book, I started to read, without comprehension. I was certainly not in a prayerful frame of mind. I was simply fulfilling an obligation.

One of the lessons for the day came from the book of Proverbs. I read:

> My child, do not forget my teaching, but let your heart keep my commandments; for length of days and years of life and abundant welfare they will give you (Prv 3:1-2).

They were just words! Nothing made sense. My eyes raced over the words, mocking them. They were written thousands of years ago, and that is where they belonged! In the past! I read a few more lines, despising the antiquated language.

> Do not let loyalty and faithfulness forsake you; bind them around your neck, write them on the tablet of your heart. So you will find favor and good repute in the sight of God and of people (Prv 3:3-4).

More words! Words that had no relevance to the real world! What was the use of reading such outdated things that could not speak to what really bothered me?

Still deaf and blind, I continued to read, mindlessly, the next few lines:

> Trust in the LORD with all your heart,
>   on your own intelligence rely not;
> In all your ways be mindful of him,
>   and he will make straight your paths
>   (Prv 3:5-6, NAB).

The words leaped off the page, striking me full force! They were written for me. They were addressed to me, right now.

I hadn't the slightest doubt that those four lines were meant for me in my present mood. An earthquake! I knew this with certainty.

I stopped and read the four lines again. Gone were my thoughts of rebellion; gone was my self-pity. I wasn't thinking of the argument I had just had with my friend, nor was I any longer trying to justify my conduct to myself. I was completely absorbed with the fact that these lines spoke to me—and they were exactly what I had to hear: "Trust in the Lord with all your heart"!

Over the next week and longer, I prayed those four lines, humbled by the fact that they were spoken to me.

"Trust in the Lord with all your heart."

For the Hebrews who wrote these lines, the heart wasn't simply an organ in the chest. It was the seat of the entire emotional and volitional life of a human being. The heart included every good desire one could possibly have, nothing excluded. Trust God with every desire, the ones I believed would never be fulfilled, the unborn yet longed for desires, my thirst for justification, my need for love, my anger—simply put, everything.

"On your own intelligence rely not."

Don't rely on your own intelligence! But that was exactly what I had been doing. The word *intelligence* means "to see into." I had been depending only upon my own ability

where God walks

to see into the meaning of all that I was experiencing. That is why I became so angry at myself and everyone else.

Not to rely on my own intelligence suggests there is another criterion, another intelligence to rely upon. But how difficult it is not to believe in what one discovers for oneself! The line of scripture was urging another approach altogether, one far more humble, far more simple and filled with peace: "Trust in the Lord with all your heart."

"In all your ways be mindful of him."

I thought of all the planning I had done to avoid pain, the unguarded words which had spilled out of my mouth like poison, my thoughts of revenge—these were all my "ways," human ways, human decisions, plans, courses of action.

I was being mindful all right, but of myself, not God.

I was being told to have a mind that is filled with God, with trusting and relying upon him—then, and then only, can one escape a mind bent on avenging itself and its wounded pride.

To be mindful of God is to yield all one's ways to him, to incorporate him in one's thoughts and decisions, or at least to consult him.

Finally, I read the great promise at the close of those four lines: "And he will make straight your paths."

If I trust in the Lord, I thought (after hours of prayer), if I do so with my whole heart and with all of my desires, if I rely not simply on my own intelligence and my own way of seeing life, and if I am mindful of God in my life, God will make straight the paths of my life, which I had made crooked by my anger and need for self-justification.

Over the following weeks, I wrote into my prayer book all the things that I discovered in those four lines—and in my heart. It seemed like it was an inexhaustible treasure, something I could always dig into—and where I could always discover something new.

After a few weeks, the margins of the book were so filled up with writing that it was all but impossible to see the print!

What affected me deeply in this experience was the realization that all things work for the good of those who trust God and seek him. Nothing can separate us from that guidance—not my narrowmindedness or my fits of childishness, not my anger, not even my boast that I could go it alone and didn't need friends—nothing!

If our hearts condemn us, scripture says, let us remember there is someone bigger than our hearts (1 Jn 3:19-20).

I saw at that time that Mystery works with our faults and failures in order to sweep away the anger in our hearts, replacing it with peace and joy, and maybe even wonder.

The earthquake! And how I needed it.

sister jeanne

I first met Sister Jeanne in a card game while I was visiting a house of prayer and seminary, a place for training young women in the religious life. Sister Jeanne had already finished her training but lived in the house since she was teaching at a nearby school. She was Irish, young, pretty, and intelligent, and I lost every card game we played. There were others playing the game, but it didn't seem to matter. Somehow I was always on the losing end!

After a number of card games and informal conversations, we got to know a little bit about each other, but not too much. Jeanne was an expert at telling a good joke and had a sharp Irish wit, but our conversations never moved beyond surface talk.

One evening the two of us were sitting in a large meeting room, talking about something I can't even recall. I started to express some feelings I had about it. Rather abruptly, Sister Jeanne cut into my conversation and said: "I know where you're going and I'm not going there."

I didn't know what to think. Her words didn't make sense.

"What are you talking about?" I asked.

"You're expressing your feelings to get me to talk and express mine, and I'm not going to do it."

Without knowing it, I had opened a closed door. I felt, suddenly, like an intruder! Somewhat embarrassed, I said: "Well, I didn't know I was doing that. I was just talking. I didn't have an agenda." That was the end of the conversation—but not of our friendship. We continued to talk or play cards occasionally, but the lines were drawn and, I thought, final.

One day I found out that she was planning a trip to Ireland. I made the offhand remark that Irish sweaters were works of art, beautifully woven. When she returned from Ireland, she handed me a white, hip-length sweater she had knitted, with interlacing Celtic designs. It was a stunning gift that must have taken many hours to finish. There was obviously some kind of communication going on between the two of us! This was fortunate for me, since I needed a good sweater and liked the idea that she had made it.

We touched bases as the months passed by, but it was never by plan. It just came about that we were in the same place at the same time.

A few years went by. Our friendship continued, but it was not a high priority in my life, or in hers. It didn't demand attention, nor did it need nourishing. It was just there.

Everything changed the day I received a call from a friend of hers telling me Jeanne was in the hospital with a particularly aggressive cancer, located in an irreplaceable organ of the body. I was caught off guard by the news. I had not even known she was sick.

I drove to the hospital with a sense of urgency. Once inside the doors, I went to the main desk in the lobby and asked for Sister Jeanne's room number. I went up the elevator and down the narrow halls, till I came to the nurse's desk.

"Would it would be all right to visit Sister Jeanne?"

The nurse looked up, her eyes suddenly wide with compassion: "Father, get her to cry if you can. She's in such

where God walks

a state of shock and denial. We could tell her we were going to cut off her legs and she wouldn't blink an eye. Something is wrong. Help her if you can, will you?"

I went into the room, attempting to digest what I had heard and trying to imagine what I would find.

Sister Jeanne was lying in bed, staring up at the ceiling, her face a mask. She didn't look my way. She wasn't looking outside. She was looking within, with fear.

"Well, are you angry at God?" I blurted out. It was a bit abrupt, I admit, but it was precisely what was on my mind. Apparently it was on hers too. She was startled. She turned and looked directly at me. Then her face crumpled and the tears started to fall, fast and heavy.

"Why me?" she moaned.

I had no answer. Who does to such questions, born of fear, pain, and the imminent sense of loss?

We talked a little, but not too much since we were interrupted every few minutes by someone taking blood or adjusting tubes. In fact, so many nurses, aides, and doctors came into that room, breaking into our conversation, that I left the room, went out to the nurse's desk, and asked if I could have a piece of paper. With a heavy, dark pen, I wrote in large letters: "Do not enter without first getting permission at the nurse's desk." I then signed my name to it and hung it on the door.

It was a Catholic hospital so I could pull rank. And I did, whenever it was needed.

I visited Sister Jeanne a number of times, but she was reticent, except to say repeatedly that she didn't understand why she had the disease. She was still in a state of shock. So were her friends, since she was so active and full of life. Her sickness seemed to touch them personally, not just as a future loss, but as a threat. If she could be struck down so suddenly, who was safe?

For some time, Sister Jeanne underwent various treatments. Once she was told that the disease was in remission. Another, that it had appeared in another part of her body. Tight lipped, she bore the pain of the treatments and spoke about it to no one. Her silence seemed like a wall separating her from her friends. They felt excluded from what she was undergoing. They became painfully worried, thinking that she had no one to talk to. She did, however. As always, she spoke little about her inner feelings, but we did talk.

During one of our conversations, I suggested that she keep a small notebook to record the passages in scripture that gave her hope or courage. Apparently, she followed my advice, though I heard nothing about the book till later.

I also loaned her a book of meditations on Julian of Norwich, thinking it might be of some help. On the title page, I wrote, "Dear Sister Jeanne, don't steal this book! It belongs to a poor Jesuit."

She didn't steal it. I'm looking at it now. A card of a praying saint marks one of the meditations that appealed to her.

> See! I am God. See! I am in everything. See! I do everything. See! I never lift my hands off my works, nor will I ever. See! I lead everything toward the purpose I ordained it to from the beginning, by the same power, Wisdom and love by which I created it. How could anything be amiss?

Once, while speaking with her, I could see that she was deeply withdrawn. So, I asked her to wait for a moment, went to my room, and got a marvelous cloth doll created by a master artist. I brought the doll to Sister Jeanne and said, "Here is something for you. It's just what you need. Put it on your bed and take a good look at it every once in awhile. Her name is Jezebel."

She looked at me, certain I had just lost my mind.

What does this have to do with me? she wondered. She was appalled that I would think she would be interested in such a character—or even in a doll for that matter!

My intention in giving her the doll was to pull her out of the mood she was in. Anger or even a good difference of opinion would do it. "You know," I said, "there's a Jezebel buried inside of you. You may discover her. That would be an interesting meeting."

where God walks

"I'll never put that on my bed, never! I don't even know what gave you the idea."

As far as I know, she never did put Jezebel on her bed, but when I visited her room after she died, Jezebel was sitting near her dresser looking at the bed.

The summer after she was diagnosed with cancer, I went to Hawaii to help out in a parish. While there, I received a letter from her. In very fine handwriting, she opened up and expressed herself in a way she could never do face to face.

Dear Father B.,

It's been seven weeks today since the Dr. told me I had a malignant tumor and would have to have surgery. What an ordeal it has been—those seven weeks have been hell and at the same time I have experienced a lot of support and encouragement. I feel like I'm traveling down a road that's paved with an awesome mingling of hope and despair, courage and fear, humor and anger, and constant uncertainty.

Somewhere in scripture it says to cast all your anxieties to God because he cares for you. I find myself doubting this at times. I had a terrifying thought one day—what if I rejected God in this whole experience? I am so confused. I don't know if I'm looking for reasons for what's happening or for a relationship with God.

Brave, honest words!

Caught between hope that she would be cured and a kind of desperation that she would not, she had mood swings, sessions of anger, and perplexity—but also, at times, a great sense of peace. Once, while sitting in a quiet summer park called Mary's Grove, her anxiety ceased. She was ". . . overwhelmed with the beauty and wonder in nature. I felt a calmness I hadn't felt in weeks. I began to think that I shouldn't be looking for explanations or reasons from God. He doesn't owe me any (does he?)."

sister jeanne   107

Then she asked the question she never would have dared to ask two years earlier: "Why do you have to be so far away at this time?" I wrote back: I am just where God wants you. She later told me, with a flash of Irish wit, "That was a typical Breault response!"

The struggle continued. So, too, did the correspondence. Whenever I traveled, we wrote. Looking back on the letters, I realize, now, how much was communicated between us—and what a privilege it was.

Her struggle wasn't between her and the doctors, or the medical staff. It was between her and God. A lot was at stake as false images of God were being burned away just as the cancer was burning away her body. Perhaps God is like a fire, and Sister Jeanne was like a moth attracted to the flame, yet fearful of it, circling it in endless fascination. In her sickness, she was discovering something of God's closeness to her and his concern for her as a person. Her death would involve a transformation. I think that is why she was afraid.

Dear Father B.,

Greetings! It has been hot but bearable.

I've been doing OK since you were here. I'm still fighting the shock of the diagnosis and trying to muster up enough will to live with it. When I first learned that my liver was diseased, I thought it was the worst thing that could happen to me. It was the end, as far as I was concerned. My dreams, aspirations, my whole life was shattered. I was confused, angry, and completely out of control of my life. I didn't want to talk about my illness. I was upset, even angry, when people told me I had to talk about it. I wasn't ready.

But she did talk, at night, when she was alone. She talked to a God "who didn't seem to be there."

In trying to explain to herself why she had the disease, she felt for a time that God was angry with her and was punishing her, but she finally rejected this line of reasoning, because "deep down inside me I knew this could not be. . . ." It was a move forward! Still she kept asking, "Why me? Why this? What have I done, or not done?"

Little by little Jeanne began to focus on her anger at God, not his supposed anger at her. Occasionally, she would catch glimpses of God's love for her. They were not frequent, but they did occur, along with occasional experiences of peace.

She was struggling to accept what she couldn't change. "I have the option of taking a more aggressive form of chemo treatment or letting the disease take its course—a rather bleak thought. For now, I have to take one day at a time. . . ."

The cancer got worse. The treatments were ineffective. And Sister Jeanne tried her best to cope with what she knew would soon happen. The days were manageable, the nights were filled with fear and anxiety.

"I had another experience the night I came home from the hospital," she wrote. Feelings of anguish and loneliness were so strong that she felt helpless and wanted to give up. At night, there was no one to put on a show for, no one asking her about her health. It was then that she felt tempted to give up—and that is when she had the experience.

She had been weeping, trying to stifle the sound so she wouldn't wake up the other sisters:

> All of a sudden, after what seemed like hours, I stopped crying—everything within became calm and quiet. It was like somebody was there and lifted a big heavy weight off of my shoulders. I remember thinking—is this how the apostles felt when Jesus calmed the raging waters around them? I continued to sit in the chair, afraid to get up and turn on the light because in spite of the calm and peace I felt, there was a fear. I'm not sure what it was—maybe it was a fear of not knowing what was happening or a fear that I was losing control of my own feelings. Was it Jesus' presence?

Tight lipped, she continued to bear the pain of the treatments and spoke about her experience to no one, not even to me, except in her letters.

Finally, with dark rings under her large burning eyes, and reduced weight, she turned her life over to God. She had stayed on her feet right up to the last day. When she died, she was surrounded by a few close friends.

The desolation and grief her friends felt after Jeanne died was overwhelming. It was as though she had died without revealing her inner struggle with cancer and death, and by that fact had rejected them, locked them out of her life. They felt deprived. The strength of their feelings was a proof of how much they loved her.

After her death the notebook was found with entries made over a two-year period. They all revealed a Job-like struggle in accepting and dealing with life and death, a struggle carried on for the most part in silence. On the last page of the notebook, she wrote down passages of scripture that had meaning for her. They were not her words, yet the impact of this woman's personality and the depth of her struggle shine through what she wrote.

"It's good to pray one liners from scripture."

What followed were the "one liners" she had found helpful in her life-and-death struggle, lines she used over and over again in prayer. In them she found the deepest meaning of all.

> For surely I know the plans I have for you, says the Lord, plans for your welfare and not for harm, to give you a future with hope (Jer 29:11).

> I have loved you with an everlasting love;
> therefore I have continued my faithfulness to you (Jer 31:3).

> "Do not let your hearts be troubled. Believe in God, believe also in me" (Jn 14:1).

> Surely goodness and mercy shall follow me
> all the days of my life,
> and I shall dwell in the house of the Lord
> my whole life long (Ps 23:6).

where God walks

I can do all things through him who strengthens me (Phil 4:13).

I myself will be the shepherd of my sheep, and I will make them lie down, says the Lord God. I will seek the lost, and I will bring back the strayed, and I will bind up the injured, and I will strengthen the weak . . . (Ez 34:15-16).

"I came to bring fire to the earth, and how I wish it were already kindled! I have a baptism with which to be baptized, and what stress I am under until it is completed!" (Lk 12:49-50).

The last words in Sister Jeanne's diary were addressed to herself: "You have no future if you get locked in the present by fears—it's what you believe, your beliefs (that count)."

How she battled! Sometimes despairingly, yet always strengthened by her hope in God, a virtue that seemed so weak at times yet proved stronger and outlasted fear, sickness, and even death—it is all revealed in the following prayer-poem, one she especially liked, written on a much used and crumpled piece of paper.

The Choice

Choose life always.
Even in the presence of death.
Surrounded by selfishness—
Even deceit,
Don't yield
To cynicism—that's death!

Choose life instead,
Always, all ways,
Every sign of it.
And choose that life
Closest to you.

When your own failures
Loom large on the horizon
Of your thoughts and feelings—
Inviting you to depression—
Choose life instead!
Especially by recalling
Past moments of grace.

When others disappoint you
And are not satisfied
With who you are,
Or the way you are,
Don't give in to melancholy.
Choose life!

If you are sick,
Confused or anxious,
Don't waste your time
Being depressed—choose life!
The life within you,
Testified to
By His love and presence,
His approval.

the communion call

One summer about twelve years ago, I spent a month serving a small parish in a town by the ocean. There was nothing fancy about the town, though it did draw tourists during the summer. The people who lived there were working people, loggers, fishermen, and storekeepers. It was not unusual to see a string of logging trucks on the highway, each trucker shifting the gears up and down, depending upon the traffic and the traffic lights. When the sun went down, it seemed like the town closed down. The streets were empty and cold. The bluish glare of the street-lights highlighted the loneliness.

Part of the work of the parish priest in this town was to take communion to those who couldn't make it to church because of sickness or age. There were no eucharistic ministers, so I was on my own. It was always an experience, since some of the people had not seen a priest for some time. In some cases they hadn't received communion in so long that their connection with the church seemed all but broken.

Another part of the experience was getting to see people as they really are. People in their own homes are not dressed for church! On entering a home, it was as though I were a family member. Nothing was cleaned up, "just for father's visit."

One Monday, I got ready to go out on the communion call. There weren't many people to visit, no more than four of five stops. I telephoned first, introduced myself, then said I'd be happy to stop by at a convenient time. This particular Monday I had a new address. I drove the car up to the curb, parked it, and started toward the house. It was a nondescript house, nothing to make it memorable, except for a motorcycle *on* the porch, blocking the door to the house. It seemed a strange place to park a motorcycle! I sensed a certain disorder within the house, even before I entered.

I knocked on the door. The young man who opened it was dressed in a black leather jacket. He took one look at me, hesitated just a moment, then brushed past me, jumped onto the motorcycle, and shot down the street, both exhausts shattering the air in protest. My guess is that he was confounded at seeing a priest on his front porch. In any event, he seemed to want out and away as quickly as possible.

His mother, a thin, fragile woman, was filled with nervous energy bordering on fear. She welcomed me into the house, which was in a state of disorder. In the center of it a man was sitting in a wheelchair, slumped forward, his head almost touching his knees. The wheelchair was facing the television set, which was filling the space with little more than noise. The man bound to the wheelchair could hardly have cared. His head was tipped to the left, his eyes were closed, and he was drooling out of the left side of his mouth. He had Alzheimer's disease. This was the man to whom I was bringing communion.

His wife, through fear and ignorance, I imagined, treated me as though I were a doctor. She started reciting symptoms her husband had, different medical diagnoses and his prognosis. It was empty talk to cover her fear, perhaps, along with a conviction that communion couldn't possibly mean much to her husband in his state. I believe she was also embarrassed for me.

I tried to quiet the lady down by suggesting she sit down on the divan, since I intended to pray over her husband. I explained that I would read a passage from scripture, give him forgiveness and then the eucharist, after which we would be quiet and finish with a final blessing.

All during this time, her husband was still pointing toward the television, now mercifully turned off. He had not moved; he was still leaning forward, still drooling out of the left side of his mouth.

It was a challenge, and on the face of it, one might wonder if it was worthwhile. I wondered myself, but I was determined: he was a parishioner after all. He was sick. Why should he be deprived of the sacrament? Still, I hadn't known he had Alzheimer's disease till I entered the house.

I began by talking to the prisoner in the wheelchair: "Jack, I'm going to give you the eucharist, but first I'd like to read a passage from scripture, ask for God's pardon, then we'll say the Our Father together. After that, I'll give you holy communion. Then we'll take a few moments for thanksgiving."

I talked to him in such a way that an onlooker might think the sick man really understood what I was saying. His wife looked on and wondered. But she remained quiet.

I went through the whole rite without any reaction from the man in the wheelchair. When it came time to give him the eucharist, I broke the bread in half and dipped it in water, then put it into his mouth. After that I sat down and told him we would be silent for a few moments and then I would say a final prayer.

We were silent. Within I felt that I had done my duty, despite any misgivings I had had about his ability to comprehend what was going on. After the silence, I said out loud a prayer of thanksgiving. I was making it up, hoping it somehow made sense, though I must admit I thought I was talking to myself. I said something like this: "Jack, it is so difficult to go through what you are suffering, very difficult. I don't understand it, nor do I have an explanation for it, except to say that it's somehow connected to the suffering of Christ, our Lord. Still, it's so difficult to do."

Suddenly Jack sat bolt upright in his wheelchair. He stopped drooling and looked directly into my eyes, opened his mouth, and said quite clearly and distinctly: "And I am doing it, Father!"

I was startled, speechless! Then, just as suddenly, he slumped back down into the wheelchair, closed his eyes, tilted his head to one side, and began to drool again out of the side of his mouth.

Was it just one moment of lucidity and awareness? Or had he understood all along? How did he come back at precisely that moment? And where had he been? Was he alone or with someone?

I later read a passage from a book titled *Why Do We Suffer?* by Daniel Liderbach. It seemed to throw a little light on this experience. "Numinous" is a word that was coined by Rudolf Otto in his seminal book, *The Idea of the Holy*. Otto had need of a word to refer to those occurrences within human experience that cannot be attributed to any known cause. He selected the Latin word numen, which conventionally has been translated as "the Divine." Otto used the Latin word to fashion a new adjective, "numinous."

This word, "numinous," Otto then used to refer to those occurrences within human experiences that cannot be attributed to known causes. The word came to mean: the Divine presence active within human experience.

Surely this moment with Jack was a numinous experience!

where God walks

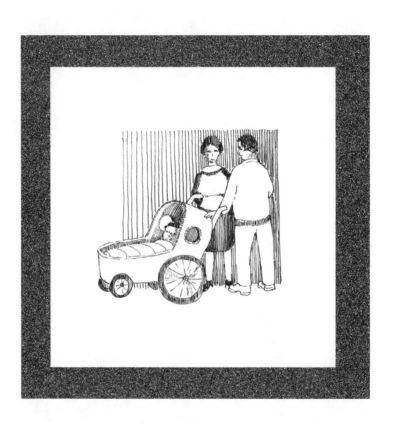

chapter 18

the adventure

Gilbert Keith Chesterton, a well known nineteenth-century literary figure, once asked the question of why some people have spiritual adventures and others don't. Then he gave his own explanation: those people have spiritual—even Divine—adventures, he said, who don't look upon life as a commodity to consume, to regulate and control. Because they don't, they are more open to what happens to them during the day. Since so many people are preoccupied with crossing off checklists of things that must be done during the day, there is hardly room in their lives for an adventure!

Chesterton explains that a Divine adventure is an intrusion into our order of the day, but one which is prayerfully considered and accepted. It is however, an intrusion, something which we didn't expect, for which we were unprepared. It is not part of our agenda. Some people react to such an intrusion by ignoring it, passing it by. Others see the invitation in it.

The following letter is an example of just such an adventure that was accepted and reflected upon. It was written by a professional woman, aloof—not from pride but from a certain modesty that prevents her from prying into other people's affairs. Nevertheless, she is very observant of what goes on around her.

I wish to explain something that happened that I shall not easily forget. During the lunch hour, I had gone to the bank from where I work. I was walking with a friend, and from the office it's a pretty good distance. Since it was Friday and the beginning of the month, it seemed like the whole world was on the street.

Right in back of us was a young man about thirty years old, thin, and not very tall, about five feet, perhaps. He was very well dressed with well combed blonde hair, and he was pushing a baby carriage. The baby was crying. The young man stopped the carriage and lifted the baby in an attempt to calm it. From where I stood—I had stopped and turned when I heard the child crying— the baby seemed tired and even sick. But what surprised me was that this beautiful blonde baby was crippled. He had small thin arms and legs, and his fingers were twisted out of shape. He was the size of a very young child—but he had all his teeth! He was at least five years old!

When I saw the child, I wanted to take him into my arms and care for him. I would like to have taken the child with me because I deeply felt that God was looking at me rather curiously through the child's eyes, which were filled with tears.

In some ways the experience was a bit unnerving. I can't wipe it out of my mind. I didn't think the child was neglected, for the father obviously loved his son.

Quite suddenly I found myself praying right there in the midst of all those people. It's as though I were somewhere else, so absorbed was I in the experience of that child.

Most people would simply have given the child a passing glance and walked on, forgetting it. However, for this woman it became an adventure. She took time to observe it, to reflect on its meaning, to go below mere surface

where God walks

details—in fact she saw in the child the mystery of Christ himself present in suffering, which drew from her spontaneous prayer. She knew of no other response.

She was on sacred ground.

The Spirit within us brings about the adventures Chesterton spoke about, the many ways in which our paths cross, without quite knowing how, or why.

touched by God
through reading

Gilbert Keith Chesterton, an English writer who lived from 1874 to 1936, was a genius known affectionately as GKC. His enormous bulk, loose fitting clothes, shaggy hair, and the pince-nez perched out on the end of his nose were his trademarks in English and European literary circles, as well as targets for cartoonists. Books by his friends line our library shelves: George Bernard Shaw, H. G. Wells, Thomas Hardy, George Meredith, Frank Sheed, and Maisie Ward. To some, Chesterton seemed filled with an optimism they neither shared nor understood. To me, he always seemed bigger than life, filled with it, and constantly communicating it to others, especially in his writing and his conversations with friends. For that reason I include this final chapter in my book, for one can certainly be touched by God in reading.

Chesterton's friends were correct about his optimism: he spent sixty-two years looking for ways of thanking God for the great gift of life. If anything characterizes his writing—and he certainly was prolific—it is the optimism and gratitude he felt. He never got over the delicious shock and wonder that he did exist—and he didn't have to! How good of God to have thought of him, to have called him into existence. Never mind the failures. Never mind the social problems his generation faced—which he addressed. Never mind even death! He was alive!

Chesterton believed that what one looks for in life is what he or she will find. And he was looking for ways of expressing his gratitude, ways of giving, not getting.

There was only one kind of person for whom Chesterton had little tolerance: the pessimist—the kind of person who finds fault with everything in life, finally rejecting the gift, along with the cosmos itself, as a hopelessly mixed up puzzle. To such a person he made this reply:

> A cosmos one day rebuked by a pessimist replied, "How can you who revile me consent to speak by my machinery: Permit me to reduce you to nothingness and then we will discuss the matter." Moral: You should never look a gift-universe in the mouth.

GKC was a versatile thinker, ready to write an informed opinion on anything or anyone. His attitude toward life spilled out into quick, animated sketches, poetry, novels, newspaper articles, books, and long conversations. God was the giver, and he, Gilbert Keith Chesterton, was the gift, which he enjoyed immensely along with all the other gifts given to him.

In one of his poems, he projects his own attitude into the thoughts of a child waiting to be born. The child promises anything, everything!—to get the great gift of life: "They should not hear from me a word of selfishness or scorn if only I could find the door, if only I were born."

It was inconceivable to Chesterton that the child would come into the world, then turn into a pessimist! That would be to go back on its promise. So it must, according to that promise, accept the world with all its puzzles, its contradictions and beauty—even the fact that it is so fleeting.

For every objection the skeptic raised, Chesterton had a response. The skeptic said: "We are dust! The whole of the earth merely a soap bubble. Life is fleeting." Chesterton replied: "Are we all dust? What a beautiful thing dust is, though. This round earth may be a soap-bubble, but it must

where God walks

be admitted there are some pretty colors in it."

He refused to be negative. "What is the good of life? It is fleeting," the skeptic asked.

"What good is a cup of coffee? It is fleeting. Ha! Ha! Ha!" Chesterton responded.

It requires a lot of care and worry to maintain a name, security, importance, and wealth. And once we get a small corner on some of these things, we are as likely as not to look to ourselves in gratitude. At that point we become rich, in the gospel sense, for all gifts come with the first gift. And that comes from God.

Scripture says, "Cast all your care on the Lord for he cares for you" (1 Pt 5:7). To do so is to know the difference between thinking you earned your own existence and knowing it is a gift. The person who knows it is a gift is a poor man, for he has cast all his care on the Lord by his gratitude. Chesterton was a poor man. He could trust God with the care of his life and still keep a contagious sense of humor. In fact, the sense of humor seemed to follow upon his act of trusting God.

In a letter to his wife after someone dear to him had died, Chesterton wrote: "Here dies another day during which I have had eyes, ears, hands and the great world around me and tomorrow begins another. Why am I allowed two?"

William Breault, a member of the Society of Jesus, is the author of eight books and numerous audio cassettes on prayer and reflection. He is the Historical Archivist for the Diocese of Sacramento, California, and Artist and Writer in Residence with the Jesuit Community there.